1-6-75

THE PSYCHIC SENSE

The Psychic Sense

PHOEBE D. (PAYNE) *Bendit*

and

L. J. BENDIT

A QUEST BOOK
Published under a grant from The Kern Foundation

THE THEOSOPHICAL PUBLISHING HOUSE
Wheaton, Ill., U.S.A.
Madras, India / London, England

First published in England 1943 by Faber and Faber Limited, London

Reprinted 1946

Revised edition 1958

Copyright © 1958 Phoebe Daphne Bendit
Laurence John Bendit
Quest Book paperback edition 1967, published by special arrangement with Faber and Faber Limited by The Theosophical Publishing House, Wheaton, Ill., a department of The Theosophical Society in America.

Second Quest Book printing 1970
SBN: 8356-0034-3
Library of Congress Catalog Card Number 67-7911

Manufactured in the United States of America

CONTENTS

PREFACE
TO THE SECOND EDITION

This book was first written during the darkest hours of the Second World War. It was not only our first joint effort at bringing together material arising out of two very different minds, it was also, we believe, a first attempt at studying psychic sensitivity from the joint angles of first-hand experience and of psychotherapy.

Since that time, now over fifteen years ago, it is not surprising if we have found that much needed restating. The original principles and the cases illustrating them seem to stand as firmly now as they did then, but the perspective on them is different—as indeed it should be after so long a lapse of time. For it is ever so, that facts and basic principles, if they are sound, remain; but the link between them, as perceived through the mind of the student, must of necessity change if the individual has allowed himself to follow the essential law of life, which is growth and change.

As a consequence, there have been a number of important alterations in the text of this edition, more especially in the earlier chapters. It is surprising how little we felt the need to change the later ones, and particularly the last, dealing with the relative values of perception and true insight. Where psychic perceptivity is concerned, much that is new has emerged in placing this function in the

9

PREFACE

fabric of the human mind and its central core of consciousness. And, moreover, the relation between what is perceived psychically at its own level and its translation into waking consciousness has undergone considerable transformation.

Many correspondents have written to us after reading the first edition. Some of course were critical, others merely wanted to tell us of their own experiences, thinking that they must of necessity be of interest to others; but many have said that the book helped to explain certain things of which they had been aware but for which they had not been able to find any adequate explanation. We hope that the present exposé may add to the number of the latter.

At the same time, nobody can be more conscious than ourselves of the fact that there can be no final answer to any problem concerning unfolding life and awareness. Indeed, it seems that the more one knows, the greater one's experience, the more there is still to be learned. That this is so is no dismal picture of the kind which dismays children when faced with the idea of 'For ever and ever and ever. . . .' On the contrary, it promises that life need never become boring because there are no further worlds to conquer. The reverse of boredom is the case, as it does not take physical strength and young vigour to delve into the mystery of life, and the deeper one goes into that mystery, the more fascinating and exciting it becomes.

P.D.P.
L.J.B.

FOREWORD
by L. A. G. Strong

This book is the result of an unusual collaboration. Dr. Bendit is a practising psychiatrist; Miss Payne is a clairvoyant. They are also man and wife.

Clairvoyants as a rule tend to be inarticulate or over-voluble. Such account of their faculties as they give does not help anyone who wishes to study those faculties scientifically. What they perceive is presented to them as vividly as the normal objects of sense perception, and they are therefore impatient of any question as to its nature and reality.

Miss Payne, however, possesses a critical mind and considerable powers of detachment. As readers of her own book[1] will realize, she has her special faculty in far greater control than the majority of psychically gifted people. She possesses it, and can now turn it on and off at will. It does not possess her. In her own language, she is a positive, not a negative psychic. This collaboration, then, with a qualified medical man, who must approach her conclusions from a widely different angle, and subject them to a professional scrutiny, has great possibilities. It has not been easy, for Miss Payne is not wholly free from the clairvoyant's belief that what is real to her must therefore be objectively real, and, of all lingoes and jargons, the pon-

[1] *Man's Latent Powers* (Faber and Faber Ltd.).

11

derous and imprecise verbiage of the psychologist is least suited to the butterfly lightness and clarity, the agonized murk of psychic perception. But the work has been done, the arguments pursued, the chapters written and re-written: and the result, I think, is valuable.

II

Comment by a layman upon a qualified medical man, if not improper, is unhelpful. I will merely say of Dr. Bendit that he is sympathetic, shrewd, extremely perceptive, and passionately interested in his profession. I have been a fellow member of more than one group and study-circle, and have had opportunities over several years to assess his mind and personality. An analyst of the school of Jung, he has something of the master's flexibility and freedom from dogma. Best of all, he is consciously and all the time a learner.

Of Miss Payne, who has no sort of medical qualifications, I can speak more freely. Her clairvoyance takes many forms, of which the most immediately useful is the power to see into people's bodies and minds. She can 'see' what is wrong with a person, physically, mentally, and psychically. She can detect and diagnose a lesion or morbid condition, and in the latter case can 'see' at a glance whether its origin is nervous or organic, and describe the nature of his derangement. She can also 'see' and describe persons, scenes, or events associated with him. She can, in certain circumstances, 'see' persons, events, or scenes in past time. She is said to have other forms of perception which I have no means of checking; and I know no verified and substantial instance of her 'seeing' anything in the future.

FOREWORD

III

Let us take first her gift for physical diagnosis. A number of medical men have made use of this, calling her in as an acknowledged or unacknowledged consultant, and can attest her power: but I will speak only of the occasions on which I have seen it at work.

1. A fellow member of one of the study-groups came in complaining that he had hit his right arm against the knob of the banisters while hurrying downstairs to join us. It was stiff and painful. Dr. Graham Howe led him to Miss Payne, with the conjuration, 'Phoebe, do your stuff.' Unhesitatingly, at a distance of five or six feet, and without uncovering the arm, she said that the sufferer had dislocated a small bone—she did not know its name, and was obliged to describe it—and would need to have it replaced. An X-ray examination the next morning confirmed this diagnosis.

2. A friend was suffering from a uterine tumour, and was shortly to undergo an operation. The tumour had been diagnosed and located, so that Miss Payne could previously have heard about it. However, on meeting the patient, she 'saw' it and exactly described its size, with one or two developments and details of which the doctors were unaware, but which were revealed at the operation, exactly as Miss Payne described them.

3. One of our cats was uneasy and crying. It lurked under the piano, and would not come out. Miss Payne said, 'It has a canker deep in its right ear.' The canker was found and dealt with.

4. Miss Payne 'saw' and diagnosed a mild infection of the urinary tract, urged the victim to go to bed, and, to his wife, foretold the time, a week, that he would lie there. (He was there a week: but this could have been a guess.)

Later, though pain and external inflammation persisted, she affirmed confidently that the infection had gone, and that the trouble was now nervous only. This verdict was confirmed by a specialist, and the patient, resuming his activities in spite of considerable discomfort, soon recovered.

5. Miss Payne arrived one day and said, 'My dear you've got neuralgia. The pain is going like this'—sketching the aggrieved nerves with her fingers. 'It's a tooth. This one.'

'Is it a goner, Phoebe? Will it have to come out?'

'Not yet. It's a goner, all right, but it will clear up this time. There's a tiny red spot under one of the roots——' and she described it precisely. 'But don't worry. It'll last you a few months yet.'

The tooth was important, since it served as a peg for a plate. I consulted my dentist, and told him exactly how I obtained the information. He was so much impressed as to change the clasp on my plate to another tooth. In five months' time the tooth blew up again. I gave it a week, then had it out. Miss Payne's diagnosis was stated by the dentist to be correct.

6. A friend was troubled by a septic tonsil. His doctor wished to remove it. Miss Payne said the poison came from a tooth, and the tonsil was not septic *per se*. The tooth was removed, and the tonsil quickly returned to normal.

A seventh instance is negative. Called in to a bad and obstinate case of rheumatism, which the doctors at last declared to be psychological in origin, Miss Payne diagnosed a minute displacement of a vertebra. An X-ray photograph, two months later, failed to show any displacement. More than one doctor has since assured me that it might well fail to do so: but there is no evidence that Miss Payne was right.

FOREWORD

IV

Of Miss Payne's power to 'see' into the mind I have abundant and in some cases embarrassing evidence. It is, however, worthless to anyone else, since one end of it depends on my assertion. But I have known her 'see' and describe a person, many miles distant, who was at the time anxious about someone in the room—all particulars subsequently verified. She has described, on being given a small wallet belonging to a girl in a town two hundred miles away, the girl, her character, her capabilities, her chief danger in life, and the nature of a crisis through which she was then passing. And she one afternoon broke off a conversation to describe the dress and appearance of an old man ('He's not alive. He's been out of the body for thirty years or more.') whom she saw passing with bowed head up and down a path in our garden. I could see no old man, nor knew of any: but inquiry among our older neighbours produced the information that just such an old man had lived here thirty years before, that he looked and dressed like that, and that he used to pace up and down this particular piece of the garden.

I have thus a certain amount of *prima facie* evidence suggesting that Miss Payne in fact possesses the powers which she claims.

V

These powers, however interesting and exceptional, have of course no direct therapeutic value. Were they her sole equipment, Miss Payne would be no more than a valuable and unusually consistent medium. But the possession of them, and especially of those which enable her to discern psychic as different from psychological states and ailments, has led her towards a secondary power, whereby she can reach and help those who suffer from such ailments. Over a period of years spent in treating patients, some of whom have been sent her by psychiatrists some of whom have come to her of themselves, she has acquired a hotch-potch of knowledge which this book is a preliminary attempt to weigh and to collate. To describe it as a hotch-potch is not to disparage it. By its nature, it must be fragmentary. It is based on pioneer work, in that shadowy hinterland between the terrain of the psychologist and those huge and formless regions which lie beyond.

Is there such a hinterland? Do such regions lie beyond? That, for many readers, will be the major challenge of this book. Miss Payne and Dr. Bendit tell us that there is such a land, and that now and then we all visit it. They seek to sketch a first geography of it, and to establish principles which will make our visits less involuntary, more frequent, and more profitable.

To use another vocabulary, they say:

(a) That most people have what are commonly called psychic powers;

(b) That those powers are real, and concerned with definite realities;

(c) That, for our health, both psychic and bodily, the more we can consciously direct those powers, the better.

They contend that the worldly distinction between objective and subjective, between material things apparent to everybody and personal things apparent only to the individual, holds good on the psychic side, in that world of which we are for most of the time unconscious. And it is here, in diagnosing the nature of psychic ill health, and seeing whether its cause is real or illusory *in its own world*, that Miss Payne's special gifts are valuable, and enable her to treat the patient with certainty and an authority outside the range of the orthodox psychiatrist.

VI

Like so many others, I have from childhood been bumped against phenomena and faculties which are inexplicable in the terms of material science or of a materialistic psychology. The tendency of my scientific friends has been to say that I am deluded, and that the phenomena, etc., do not exist. I might perhaps have been tempted to agree; but if ever I averted my eyes, circumstances stepped in and rubbed my nose in the offending subject until I gave it due attention. Slowly, over years, I acquired my own small hotch-potch of unrelated experiences, and struggled to assimilate them into the faith by which I live. The result has been insignificant, but I know that I must at no time abandon the endeavour: and, to me, the work of Miss Payne, and, especially, this first joint statement of it, have been extraordinarily helpful. It has lit for me several dark places, and has enabled me to bring into conscious focus much that lay around the eye's corner. Above all, it has given me that creative nudge which makes us suddenly see a way for ourselves.

I commend it therefore to anyone who believes that man has a twofold nature and existence, who is interested in the interaction of mind and body, and who has ever stopped to ask, 'Now how on earth did I know that?'

VII

The authors' approach to their difficult subject is straightforward and courageous. They reveal, naturally, a bias in favour of the acute and commanding perceptions which they know so well, and the immaterial bucket sometimes sends the material bucket ignominiously sky high: but truth is obtained by yielding to one's natural bent as often as by discounting it. Miss Payne, and, more surprisingly, Dr. Bendit seem to me to underrate the objection that the forms seen by a medium, even though constant, may be contributed by the medium and may not be proper to, or even symbolic of, the reality which is being perceived. But so elementary an objection can be provided by the reader, and need in no vital way vitiate the book's general conclusions.

One last word. The book's subject matter, though it calls for systematic and careful study, is not yet susceptible of the kind of proof that would be demanded in a laboratory. The authors know this and acknowledge it frankly. They are making a personal statement, and since to have qualified every sentence with 'it seems as if' or 'it appears as though' would have cumbered their text, they have ventured, wherever possible, on the simpler form 'it is'.

CHAPTER I

Discovery

One of the characteristics of the Western mind is scepticism. Another is inquisitiveness. These qualities, used singly, would inevitably lead to frustration, for unbelief without further enquiry is purely negative, while inquisitiveness without the ability to doubt leads to credulity. Together, however, they are a powerful team and, indeed, may be said to have given to the West the technical ascendancy which it has had—and is now losing —over other peoples.

At the same time, scepticism has destroyed much where moral and spiritual values are concerned. In the nineteenth century it made a great deal of old superstition untenable, but replaced it by a new superstition, that of positivism and materialism on which science is said to depend. In the process, however, much that is of worth has been lost or at least obscured. Spiritual values are in reality ineradicable, and reflect profound intuitions on the true nature of man and his relation to the world in which he lives.

Among other things which are shunned and decried by modern science is the age-old belief in visions, in 'psychic' and magical powers, in the existence of other worlds besides the physical, and the ability of man to contact them. Man is said to have five senses, showing him the physical world, and that is all. Anything else falls into the realm of illusion and delusion, and is associated with morbid mental states. It is only in the last twenty years or so that, once more, attention has been turned to these phenomena, not as erratic, occasional events, but as things capable of observation and study, to be linked with the science of psychology which is now firmly founded if not equally soundly developed.

For many people, in the course of their lives, have dramatic instants of vision in which the everyday, material world loses its importance. Attention is for the moment focused at another level where objects and people appear to have an impact and quality often rightly described as 'other worldly'. Such experiences have an effect on the viewer which is quite different from that of ordinary events.

It may be that the vision is momentary, blinding and transforming to the beholder: such a one has been described by Warner Allen in *The Timeless Moment*. It has then much in common with the ecstatic experiences of saints and mystics. Again, it may be that the vision is realized as symbolic and significant only to the beholder, and represents a dramatization of his own state of mind. Or it may be that it is of some person, or of some scene remote from where one is, but eventually proved to be veridical. It may be that explicit foreknowledge of some coming event is given; or, looking backwards in time, that a reproduction of the past is seen.

More frequently, however, certain people find themselves subject to indefinite feelings and promptings whose source and origin cannot be traced, as for instance when in the periods of half-light at dawn and at dusk the everyday world seems to become transformed into strange and fascinating shapes. Ugly things soften their outlines and sink into a background of subtle shades. Ordinary objects become invested with a new grace, and, for a brief spell, acquire certain transient qualities which fade once more into practical realities as morning breaks, or darkness falls and blots them out.

Some people find that half-light either alluring or frightening, and in either case are liable to lose their ordinary sense of proportion; while others accept these times as part of the day's cycle and think no more about them. This is because these periods of between-lights have a strange affinity with the psychic world, and to those who are familiar with extra-sensory perception there is nothing unnatural about this affinity, any more than there is about the dawn and the dusk in the physical world.

What exactly happens at this point? Why should a half-light—a few moments of transition—be more puzzling than darkness in which one sees nothing or daylight in which there is so much to be seen? It is because of a change from one phase to the next, in which values shift. Certain physical characteristics are lost, colour is replaced by black and grey, well-known outlines fade into the general mass of shadow, and new perspectives emerge as night or day take command. Yet these new and passing values are not merely products of imagination. They are just as real as those of daylight. It is as if, while the scene is being changed from day to night, one had a glimpse of another world behind the familiar stage. This backstage world is in every way as valid as that immediately behind the footlights. Those from whom the world of the theatre holds no secrets know that the real life of it takes place out of sight of the crowd, and that the play itself is only the outermost phenomenon of a large and complex scheme. It is the same with the psychic background to physical and psychological life.

An increasing number of people vaguely sense the truth of this. And indeed, there are some who are so anxious to try and develop 'psychism' or 'sensitivity' that they embark on courses for development or training without any notion of what the cost may be, whether in money, possible injury to themselves, or frustration. Others, wiser and more cautious, hold back, though they feel the need for some kind of a lead as to how to set to work. They may know that they have probably got some sort of extra-sensory perceptivity, but they do not know how to set about understanding it and themselves in regard to it.

It is for that reason that this book has been written.

To most Western people, the easiest and most natural approach to the discovery of personal psychic faculties is the psychological. This is because psychology is an outcome of the scientific method of the West. Western science rose out of the urge to know accurately about the phenomena taking place around us, and its methods have naturally followed a course which satisfies that urge, and which harmonizes with the particular pattern of the Western mind. Psychology represents the adaptation of this method to the field of the mind itself; and the development represented by introspective analytical methods, is an attempt to push the method still further, and for the scientist to study his own mind from within itself. Yet, even analytical methods of psychological study have largely failed to recognize and accept psychic perceptivity as a direct and normal part of human experience. Nor has any other line of scientific investigation filled the gap and linked together the results of psychical research and the everyday life of everyday people. It is clear, however, that if people have psychic capacities in their make-up, a complete grasp of the nature and structure of the mind must include them and put them in their right light and place in that structure. For as all sound psychologists recognize, one can only deal with things by learning to see them as they really are: that is, from all angles, both subjective and objective, both personal and impersonal. This applies to psychic experience as to everything else. It is, as we have said, on psychic or extra-sensory perceptivity, considered as a window opening on to a real world outside one's own mind, that we wish to dwell in these chapters.

The question to be answered is, 'If I have these extra-sensory faculties and they are active even though I do not know it, how can I set about finding them and making them conscious?' There are already two well-known avenues of general research, the one represented by the modern spiritualistic movement, the other by such scientific bodies as The Society for Psychical Research and the academic circles which study the subject under the name of parapsychology. A third and more personal line is that suggested in this book, which is that of careful analysis of one's own experience, somewhat on the lines of analytical psychology.

Apart from the fact that this third line is more intimate and can be carried out without elaborate equipment, there is a fundamental difference between the purpose to be achieved by it and the aim of the other two. Spiritualism, for instance, covers a wide field. It ranges from many forms of primitive phenomena, through mediumship, lectures, and classes, to a high type of ethical philosophy with a marked religious background. But the general tendency among members of spiritualistic movements has in the past been rather to *allow* things to happen than to discover *how* they happen and *why*. They have been chiefly concerned with 'communications' and did not aim at understanding how or whence they come. Fortunately this uncritical attitude has begun to alter to one rather more bjective. Psychical Research and the parapsychologists, on the other hand, are concerned with the investigation of evidence in an endeavour to discover whether, and under what conditions, psychic phenomena occur at all. The line of approach is impersonal and objective, entails much painstaking observation, collation of evidence, and the elimination of possible error by rigid check on every experiment.

Valuable as this work is, it tends to lack the human element, and so gives an impression of being academic, remote and sterile.

There are at least three ways of achieving the object of the third method, that of seeking and analysing experience of our own and of investigating our own faculties:

1. The use of artificial assistance. This overlaps on to the field of spiritualism.
2. Yoga.
3. Observation and study of the psychic background of experience, both in the past and in the present.

1. History tells us that there have always been crystal-gazers, geomancers, augurs, and soothsayers of many kinds, who use some form of apparatus which excites or stimulates psychic activity. Such means are legion and include sand-divining, card-reading, teacup-reading, planchette, automatic writing, and all the lesser occult arts. The apparatus used mostly serves one purpose, and that is to act as a focus through which the psychic function is concentrated. The deliberate concentration of attention necessary to read cards or look into a crystal produces in the operator a very slight degree of self-hypnosis. The

result is not actually to increase the psychic powers of the medium but to give them more prominence by decreasing the degree of attention focused on the physical world immediately about him. That is, there is a relative increase in psychic clarity because the focus of attention is shifted. What occurs is that the medium develops a habit of easy dissociation, thereby losing his normal close touch with the material environment. In this way he becomes more open to conscious psychic experience and aware of impulses reaching him from the psychic world. In reality, he is half-way between two worlds, and his consciousness stands precariously on a flimsy bridge between them. The instability of this foothold explains the uncertainty and often dubious veracity of many 'communications', and explains why these messages are often a jumble of unintelligible and at times frankly nonsensical matter with, here and there, a very pertinent point jutting out.

W. B. Yeats used to speak of a half-way condition which occurs between full waking consciousness and hypnosis, in which the subject finds disconnected images flashing through the mind one after another. These phantasmagoria, as he terms them, appear to be comparable to the isolated beads and pieces of coloured glass in a kaleidoscope: when they are fixed, either in a waking state or in sleep, they form a pattern; but in the intermediate phase, when one pattern has dissolved and before another is formed, they become a cascade of individual and unrelated bits. On analysis, they will be seen as a mixture of fragments of psychological material out of the subject's own mind and of scraps of psychical perception. The 'communications' of mediums are often something of the same kind of jumble, but one step more coherent.

The objection to the use of apparatus to focus the attention is that it involves a process which, instead of leading towards a greater degree of integrity, control, and self-awareness, such as is our goal to-day, works in the reverse direction. It induces a tendency, as the mediumship develops, to a greater degree of unconscious activity and to a splitting, not a knitting together, of the parts of the personality. Many, however, rely upon methods involving paraphernalia, and will legitimately continue to use them because they give the results they are looking for.

We, however, are concerned here with studying the natural growth of psychic perception rather than with methods comparable to forcing a plant, with the result that it can only function under hothouse conditions. The use of apparatus may enable us more easily to perceive things in the unseen worlds, but it does not teach us anything about our own psychic sensitivity or the way it behaves. As to the use of drugs, such as mescalin, it need scarcely be said that they are harmful, and a very undesirable way of opening up contact with the unseen. Their regular use inevitably leads to deterioration of the personality and leaves the subject a victim to the unpleasant and often terrifying sights of the psychic hinterland, as in the case of opium addiction and delirium tremens.

2. There has of late years been a vogue for rather glib books on breathing exercises and certain types of yoga designed for the purpose of stimulating psychic powers. These will certainly bring about results if properly and assiduously performed. But unless these exercises are recognized for what they are, and seen as part of a wide system of self-training, they may be very dangerous and lead to loss of self-control and sense of proportion. In their own setting, these systems are really only one part of a comprehensive scheme of spiritual education known in India as Raj Yoga, or Royal Yoga. The purpose of this is

to lead the aspirant to enlightenment concerning himself and his relation to the universe. Breathing exercises in this scheme are comparable to gymnastics. Simple deep breathing is essential to maintain a flow of physical vitality, while long, quiet breaths help to steady the mind so that it does not waver or blur the images of what is being observed. On the other hand, many modes of breathing at present being popularized can prematurely burst the sheath of budding faculties and cause both physical and psychic injury. The various schools of Raj Yoga give us schemes complete in themselves, not only for discovering the psychic and psychological but also the spiritual nature.

It would seem, however, that what is called Yoga in India has also been practised in various forms by other races and the followers of many faiths. Investigations of Maori practices or those of the highly cultured Chinese show that methods differ considerably in accordance with different racial cultures. Aryan India, as the cradle of the Indo-European race, has initiated and prescribed methods which would appear to be most suited for Anglo-Saxon use. Yet even the methods of the Hindu Brahmin of the highest type are such that the European and American would, in many cases, find them difficult to apply in detail. While the principles stand, the details need to be adjusted to the Western temperament. For example, the Hindu meditates cross-legged on the floor, in what is to him a natural sitting position. While some Westerners find this easy, most find it exceedingly uncomfortable, and it is an axiom that one can only meditate effectively if physically at ease. To insist on such a detail is to lose the substance for the shadow, and probably to make useful meditation impossible.

Further, the Western mind, by virtue of its training, has reached a certain point in scientific objectivity. The modern cult of introspective psychology turns that objectivity on to ourselves and attempts to study ourselves and our subjective experience with the same detachment as one would apply to a bird in the hedge. The Hindu yogi is doing the very same thing, but his background is different, in that his training gives him something which we have not, although it does not give him the particular thing which is characteristic of the West. His background is mystical and religious, that of the West materialistic. His, though possibly more exalted, has the practical disadvantage of being vague and nebulous as to material things, while the Western outlook, though perhaps more mundane, has the virtue of clarity, punctuality, and sharp focus. This clear definition is a great asset to the occidental mind and is his means of self-discovery.

These, then, are the reasons why we are approaching the subject from the standpoint of modern psychology rather than by the old traditional route. The difference between the psychic and the psychological approach is, however, that the former insists, because of the observed form of its perceptions, on coupling with a study of the psychological phenomena a picture of them as objective and material occurrences. These are comparable with what happens when a person walks from one place to another or moves a chair across the room; so that when one considers a person filled with sullen hatred and he succeeds in transforming that hatred into constructive affection, there appears to be not only a psychological change but an actual and material change in the fabric of the psychic organism as well.

3. The method of investigation proposed here involves neither the need for apparatus nor breathing exercises. Indeed, it requires no artificial stimulus of any kind, only healthy curiosity. Yet, as was emphasized earlier, no use-

ful results can be hoped for unless this curiosity is coupled with a willingness to detach oneself from preconceptions and to see oneself as one is rather than as one would like to be. This is essential to anybody who wants to learn to disentangle psychological material from extra-sensory perceptions, and to assess both at their true value. If he is not sufficiently detached in his attitude to himself there is a danger that he will rid himself of the responsibility for unacceptable ideas which really emanate from his own mind, by considering them as coming from the external psychic world. This is scarcely likely to lead to objective results. Moreover, there is usually nothing sensational or dramatic in psychic perceptions. On the contrary, the investigator must be prepared to look at commonplace rather than rare things: the only dramatic quality about the investigation lies in seeing things in a new light and in discovering a new world for experiment and investigation.

Most people find that when uncanny things are being discussed they can recall some similar event in their own experience. Some have been in haunted houses, others have had strange premonitions, or have seen or dreamed vividly of some episode taking place at a distance. But these incidents are almost always exceptional and sporadic. The discovery of one's own psychic nature is usually much more casual and, most likely, simply means that one comes to realize that something one has known or done all one's life is due to the activity of unsuspected faculties. To see a ghost would be a red-letter day event to most people, but to discover that one is in direct daily touch with another world without having suspected it is far more startling if suddenly realized. Molière's hero got far more pleasure out of discovering that he had spoken prose all his life than he would have from his first production of an essay in the literary form called prose. His experience, moreover, emphasizes two other points which are important where psychic experience is concerned: in the first place, his discovery impressed nobody but himself, though to him it meant a lot; secondly, it was only because his teacher of grammar pointed it out that he saw that his everyday speech was couched in a literary form with a name to it.

Many people have extra-sensory experiences of which they are conscious, but they do not make any mental link between these and the term 'psychic'. In fact, there are some who shun the word because of its associations with pseudo-mysticism. Dunne, for instance, vigorously denies anything psychic in his precognitive dreams, and yet both in these and in his other experiments he is discussing phenomena which belong entirely to what is commonly called the world of psychic phenomena.

For one who decides to undertake this kind of investigation it is useful to begin his study with a quiet retrospect on early years. There the student will almost certainly find some event which sticks in his mind and seems outstanding for no immediately obvious reason. If he tries to find the reason, one of two things is likely to become apparent: either the event represented a psychological crisis, the culmination of a series of associated occurrences after which an old pattern of feeling broke and a new one was formed; or it may be of a different nature, in which a minor physical event becomes important, not because of emotional memories, but because of the influence which it contains. This is a subtle background, immediate and self-contained, which leaves an indelible mark.

An example of the first type is where a young girl, the

daughter of parents who quarrelled constantly, suddenly changed her attitude towards them. She had previously considered her mother to be a harsh, unjust, and brutal person, and her father to be her prop and support. On her twelfth birthday, the family sat down to dinner, and the customary quarrel flared up. At this, in the twinkling of an eye, she perceived her mother as a weak, querulous, and pathetic woman, and her father as a bully. This henceforth was her feeling about them, and represented something quite different from her previous attitude. This is a simple psychological process of reviewing old material and suddenly seeing it in a new light.

The second kind of event is illustrated by the following account: 'When I was a child in my teens we went to live in a house which had been empty for some time. It was a pleasant house, and even the semi-basement was light and airy. The family settled in happily, and I particularly enjoyed the sense of spacious freedom. One day when I was alone in the basement kitchen I was suddenly aware of somebody entering the room, and at the same time I was invaded by a sense of misery and utter depression. I went very cold, and my first impulse was to fly upstairs and find company. The feeling grew so strong that finally I could bear it no longer and could not stay and finish the meal I was eating. In spite of myself I felt so desolate and miserable that I ran to the top of the house to find my parents, though I was careful not to say anything of the uncomfortable experience. Weeks after, and this time at night, I again happened to be in the kitchen alone, when once more there came this overwhelming sense of someone coming slowly through the door. This time I saw a dark shadow, which, on closer examination, proved to be a little old woman with grey wispy hair and a little grey shawl about her shoulders. She looked distraught, and the room seemed filled with miserable gloom. At that I hastily turned off the gas and made off to bed. In the morning I told my father. He was sufficiently intrigued to call upon neighbours to inquire why the house had stood empty for so long. After considerable pressure, the Baptist minister next door admitted that the last tenant, an old woman, had committed suicide by hanging herself behind the kitchen door. Her sons had grown up and gone off, she developed melancholia, and had killed herself during one of her bad spells. Neighbours agreed that the picture of the old woman given to my father tallied with their knowledge of her.'

The difference between this and the previous instance is obvious. The first story was the last incident of a continuous series, and was remarkable not because of anything new or unusual happening outside the patient but because of a change within herself. In the second, however, there were no previous associations, and the net result was not a psychological change of attitude in the observer. It was an experience as isolated and objective as if she had unexpectedly seen the old lady in the flesh walk in at the door. The old woman did not happen to possess a physical body but her psychic body appeared perfectly objectively to the one who saw it.

Sometimes, the ordinary method of psychological treatment by analysing back into the experiences of early childhood may put one on the track of psychic experience. For, as has been said, certain phenomena one remembers may stand out from the general background of the analysis, and cannot be made to fit into it in the usual way. In one case the patient described a curious sense of what he called 'slipping back' from the material world into another realm. He described it as floating away until the room and the people in it seemed far away, and he felt as though he were seeing it through the wrong end of a telescope. If he were nervous and frightened he might even see himself in the room, speaking and acting under his own control, but as if he were a puppet-master working the strings, not as if he were actually in his body. Then sometimes he slipped out altogether into a region where all physical sounds and objects were muffled in whitish-grey mist. It was not in itself an unpleasant world, because it was quiet and the scolding of grown-ups did not penetrate to it. There were no particular shapes in it, but an even, slow, drifting movement, as of wreaths of fog, in which he was the one fixed object.

Technically, and from the point of view of the psychologist, the patient was describing a state of dissociation. That is, his personality was split, and the two parts separated: a phenomenon which occurs in many conditions, including epilepsy, and 'loss of memory', or fugue. This is an easy matter to name from the psychological angle, and it is possible to explain also why it happened— that is, that it was provoked by the stress of nervousness or the boredom of being forced to sit politely on a chair, 'seen but not heard', while his mother and her cronies had all the fun and conversation.

The unexplained thing is the character of this grey world. It does not fit at all with the psychological idea of compensatory fantasy. In such a case a bored or frightened child usually goes into a world in which enforced inaction gives way to daydreams of pleasant adventure, in which he shines as a hero, or the dullness of a front parlour turns into bright, sunny fields and sea beaches. Even when it is quietness the child looks for he does not choose for himself a world of colourless mist.

The true nature of this experience only suggested itself when the patient met with Evelyn Underhill's *The Grey*

World and the writings of Algernon Blackwood. It then became obvious that his 'fantasy' was not personal to himself, but that he was conscious of a place which, if it did not exist objectively and outside himself, was at least the common property of others, too. This condition is a common experience of people with a marked psychic temperament, and is that of a half-way state where the person is neither properly in contact nor right out of contact with the physical world.

During analysis the patient realized that there were other 'places' he knew about, and which he subsequently found to be part of the experience of others besides himself. These were not linked with psychological situations like the grey world. They conveyed to him a strong sense of atmosphere, but the crisp, happy content of them lent itself readily to their being described as fantasies. Yet there was always an uneasy feeling in his mind that this explanation was at least incomplete.

Another way of securing a great deal of information as to the psychic sensitivity of our temperament is through reactions to present environment. Awareness of difference of atmosphere is most common. People speak of liking or disliking the atmosphere of a place or person, yet they never stop to analyse what they mean. Nor do they realize how often a sense of atmosphere may cut straight across material facts. Formulated, such a contrast expresses itself in phrases which fit exactly, but which are often not strictly logical. A friend who stayed in a beautiful house in the Cotswolds with cultured, artistic people explained when he came away, 'It was a lovely house, and the Y's were charming, but theirs was not a home, they were only lodgers there.' One can hear the critic exclaiming, 'What do you mean? The house has been in the family for generations, and they live there year in, year out. How can you say it is not a home?' Yet others grasp the idea at once: a subtle quality is missing which makes a house happy and comfortable and those who live in it 'at home'.

It is interesting to watch for such apparently illogical impressions about things and people. It is easier to weigh up a person than a place, because one is helped by slight changes of expression and movement. Nevertheless one may become aware of a great deal of intangible 'background' to that person, less *from* than *through* what one sees of him. It is as though the fringes of one's consciousness put out feelers and register faint but unmistakable facts about people and things, which are recorded lucidly though they have not passed through the ordinary thought processes. A unique quality of these impressions is their sense of conviction. The conviction of truth may be dislodged temporarily by rational thinking, but it will return again and in the end prove itself to be well founded.

Many a wife has been snubbed for her pains in warning her husband not to trust a certain man in business. The logical, matter-of-fact husband points out that he has excellent references, that he has laid all his cards on the table, is polite and considerate, his hospitality has been most generous. In short, she is talking nonsense. Yet in a few months the maddening, illogical woman has been in the position of being able to say, 'I told you so!' The intuitive factor is by no means a feminine prerogative, but the majority of men automatically invoke an intellectual factor which they term logical, which usually inhibits the flight of intuitive perception.

For a scientific thinker it is often necessary that he should deliberately take his mind off the material facts before him in order to understand their significance. Often, when confronted by a complex matter, we put it aside and, as we say, 'sleep on it' before the solution can be found. It is necessary to relax in order to get a clear perspective of the problem. By doing something of the same kind, and deliberately looking, not at a material happening, but at what is taking place on the fringe of consciousness and out of the circle of the limelight of direct attention, all kinds of scarcely perceptible feelings and whisperings make themselves known and tell us that the truth of the situation is not what it appears to be. We see more of it by not looking straight at it than by direct and focused attention. It needs a certain knack to do this. It is similar to the astronomer's trick of looking out of the corner of his eye at a very dim star, because he sees it better. This is because the outer edge of the retina of the eye is more sensitive to half-light than the central part, and so can see things which disappear if we look straight at them. It is the same where psychic perceptions are concerned; one is so much used to direct focused vision in the centre of the physical field that one has to teach oneself to pay attention to the fine shades which can only be perceived outside the centre. A good teacher, a capable organizer who knows how to handle people, a shrewd diplomat, and, above all, a true artist, must of necessity be capable of shifting his focus and of reading psychically both people and situations, so as to sense that which lies deeper than superficial appearances.

Yet another suggestion for practice is a careful analysis of such a thing as a day spent in the country. What is it that one has enjoyed? Is it just a blur of pleasant feeling? Was it the colours of the landscape, or the smell of the wet earth or hay, or the physical sense of well-being engendered by the warm sun and air on one's skin? Was it the thrill of life in the trees and growing things around one, the kinship with that life? Was it the atmosphere of mellow antiquity in some part of historic England, or was it the sense of remoteness from any human contact? Do individual trees seem to be friendly and others aloof or even hostile? What is it that has given us satisfaction and refreshment? We may allow our imagination to play on all these things, and see what complexities of feeling and imagery we can evoke, and whether these are psychological, reminding us of the past, or whether they are pure spontaneous perceptions.

Another avenue of exploration is to note forebodings of something which may happen, such as the feeling that one is going to have a bad day, or to have the conviction while dressing that a troublesome letter awaits one downstairs, even though there are no data for such a supposition. Then again there is the occasional intuition that we shall meet a particular person, or the sudden impression that at a special time a friend was doing some definite thing. These psychic precognitions can be made to serve a useful purpose because they give an opportunity of testing the accuracy of such experience. Mistakes are inevitable and should be frankly admitted. Better: a written record of experiments should be kept, and the results written down at once. All chance of wishful thinking can then be eliminated, and the mathematically minded can estimate his results with accuracy. In one case a woman saw a friend who lived some miles away changing from a green dress into a brown one. She was sufficiently sure of this happening to telephone the friend at once to test it, and found that she was right. Many similar occurrences confirmed her in thinking that she was markedly psychic. Reasonable expectations of such things must, of course, be eliminated. Many and various positive experiments can be made. One may pick up a letter before opening it and, without any preconceived idea as to its contents, try to get the feeling of it, and after a good many blanks one day an idea of what the letter contains may flash into the mind, and quite possibly the mood the writer was in when it was written. If one perseveres with this kind of experiment it is surprising how the field widens and how outlying details are psychometrically conveyed.

A man working in the West End of London used to leave his office in the evening and drive home, going into Hyde Park at Lancaster Gate. At one point the road forked so that he had a choice of ways to the same gate of the park. According to which way the point policeman controlling the traffic at Lancaster Gate was facing, he would be stopped for a longer or shorter time. His experiment was to try and find out which road to take on any given evening to avoid waste of time—in other words, to forecast what the invisible policeman would be doing some minutes hence. He found that if he could make what he called a 'pre-rational' decision in terms of 'Left' or 'Straight on' *before* he gave himself time to think, he was right in his choice perhaps three times out of four—in any case, in considerably more than half his journeys. In fact, he said that after a time he stopped being interested in making the right decision and was more concerned to find out what had made him make the wrong one.

In another instance, two friends were discussing a manuscript, when one said to the other, 'Mother is wanting me; she is fidgeting. I must see what she needs.'

The other replied, 'How do you know?'

'I can feel her fussing!' was the answer.

The mother was across the house, in the kitchen. As the door opened, she said, 'I have been wanting you, and was just about to call you, but I did not like to interrupt.'

These incidents are very common and trivial, but the thing seldom recognized is their implication and significance.

Yet another phenomenon is that of dreaming of something to come, or something at a distance. Dunne, already mentioned, has done justice to the precognitive dream. The other is rare but occasionally proves convincing. There are a good many cases where people have dreamed of ordinary incidents happening to their relatives or friends in other parts of the world, and in many cases these dreams have been carefully checked, allowing for differences of time, etc., as being of things actually taking place.

A curious psychic flair that a few people possess is simply knowing that a particular thing is going to happen, generally speaking, without rhyme or reason. One man always knew long in advance when people around him were going to die. He used to worry members of his family when he suddenly said, 'Oh! don't be cross with A., she will be dead within a year!' or however long it was. When it was pointed out to him that A. was hale and hearty and thoroughly enjoying life he stuck firmly to his opinion and merely remarked, 'Never mind—I know!'— and know he did, for when he spoke in such a way he was never wrong.

Clearly, one could multiply examples and suggest ways of study and experiment indefinitely, but the value of suggested methods is far less than that of those one initiates for oneself. Other people's experience is never wholly convincing, no matter how circumstantial, although it is useful to correlate such evidence and lay it alongside one's own.

If personal experience presents something suggestive of active extra-sensory perceptivity, there is encouragement to go on experimenting and investigating. At first, results are likely to be mixed, haphazard, and probably unsatisfactory. Gradually one's technique improves: a personal psychic pattern emerges out of the chaos and we learn to become more attentive to it. It does two things for us: firstly, it enriches our understanding of things by supplying a double perspective on them, the outer physical and the inner or hidden; secondly, it allows us to develop increasing control of the faculties themselves by making them conscious. This gives a greater stability to emotional life and a more balanced ability to make clear judgments and decisions in relation to subtle matters.

If an individual is concerned primarily, not with enriching his perceptions by adding to them a conscious psychic field, but rather with securing for himself reasonable comfort and emotional balance, psychotherapy alone may be all that is required. It allows the patient to follow the evolutionary path from primitive, inchoate psychism to the stage of clear, rational thinking, in which the psychic nature is obscured and overruled by the intellect. If, on the other hand, we are seeking the fullest possible comprehension of things which lie in all their aspects, then at some time or another the ability to make use of our subtle perceptivity must perforce be brought back into the picture.

If one is stable enough at once to take psychic experience into account a phase of blindness can be avoided. The psychic field is then dealt with at the same time as the psychological. Using a bi-focal vision upon both, the individual can pass by experiment and education directly from the primitive phase of automatic response, to the intelligent comprehension and direction of the personal psychic as well as the psychological life. This may bypass the intermediate phase in which one is either psychically confused or else blind altogether to this aspect of experience.

But there is another side of the matter which may not be immediately apparent, which is that if one is interested in clarity and depth of perception of ordinary, physical objects, to get one's extra-sensory perceptivity into its right place is of very real help. This matter is summed up by a correspondent who says, 'In recent years I have learned to understand something of my intuitive perception, and this has been of use to me in two ways. On the one hand, I have learned to trust it so that it is of great use in my professional work and in dealing with people. But, on the other, I have realized that in the past my physical senses lay under a cloud: they were so much mixed up with my "psychism" that they never functioned clearly.

'I now see colours and shapes, hear music and other sounds in the physical world, with a richness and depth I had never before dreamed of. Despite all the unpleasantnesses, it is now a place of constant joy and excitement where there are always new things to observe. In short, by allowing myself to become consciously in some measure "psychic" I have discovered a physical world, and know what Jung said when he told me that I had not accepted the (physical) sensation function.'

CHAPTER II

Psychic and Psychological

At the beginning of the last chapter we suggested at least three different experiences, all of which can be classed as visionary.

The first, in which a blinding moment of insight hits the mind of the beholder with some transcendental quality is one which can be termed spiritual. The word Spirit is one which will be further discussed later. The second, which is of a personal nature often involving subjective symbolism is best called psychological. But the third involves perception of situations or objects outside the range of the normal senses, and forms a category to which the term 'psychic' is colloquially applied.

We shall use the common word for its convenience. To have constantly to refer to 'extra-sensory perception' (e.s.p.), 'psychokinesis' (pk.) or 'the Psi function' is cumbersome. Moreover, the term 'sensitive' as applied to an individual is apt to be ambiguous, as many people are highly sensitive to anything affecting their own feelings and prestige, but not in the least to anything else, or of a 'psychic' nature. 'Medium', too, as applied to a perceptive person is a false quantity, not only because many psychically sensitive people are not in the least mediumistic, and in fact would strongly repudiate the term, but also because many of those calling themselves mediums have only a modicum, if any, of psychic perceptivity.

It is of the hidden world of psychic, as against psychological experience that we wish primarily to speak, because its influence, though usually unrecognized, permeates the substance of daily life and experience. If at our present stage of evolving consciousness it remains unrecognized, it seems to be the cause of problems as baffling and bewildering in their own way as those dealt with in the part of the psychological field which is concerned with analysing and studying reactions to physical experience. A psychic experience causes psychological reactions just as does a physical experience. It is axiomatic that the psychological reaction to a physical experience must be consciously related to the physical object which has provoked it, before it can be properly understood. Similarly, the psychological reaction to a psychic experience must be related to its own origin before it can be assimilated.

Psychology has explored a vast field, ranging from academic deserts to green lands of human material. But of late it seems to have undergone a cleavage. On the one hand, following the lead of C. G. Jung, an increasing number of clinicians are learning more and more of the fundamental nature of spiritual and religious urges in man. On the other, the new sub-science of cybernetics, in imitating by means of electronic apparatus the functions of the nervous system, has become capable of producing machines giving a semblance of animal behaviour. This has made many think once more that life can be explained in purely mechanistic terms. But between the two extremes there lies a field as yet barely explored which concerns the perceptive function of the mind: that function which makes the individual aware of the world outside himself—primarily the physical world, but also those other worlds already mentioned, the spiritual and the psychic.

True, scientists who have taken the trouble to investigate the matter, and who have put aside their prejudices against an uncomfortable doctrine, must now accept the evidence that man has at least a sixth sense beside the five physical ones. But the parapsychologists who have studied this, have gone little further than to establish the existence of 'Psi', a mental function which acts either as extra-sensory perception or as psycho-kinesis, according to whether it is cognitive or conative. Beyond this they know that this function does not obey the physical laws of time and space. On the contrary, they find 'time displacement effects' where, for instance, a worker gets results unrelated to an experiment in progress, but to one still to come; or they fail so positively to get results that it is evident that the mind is actively refusing to co-operate; while distance between operators makes no difference to telepathy, and emotional rapport does. None have so far gone into the question of e.s.p. or psychism as a common, everyday aspect of human behaviour and thought. Yet careful study suggests that it is an aspect of mental life which often complicates the subjective, psychological processes of people, filtering into their rational thinking scarcely noticed data about people and situations which upset their judgments and blur the clarity of their conclusions. The psychologist either steers his patient carefully round it as a dangerous area, or else deals with it, if he must, as something purely symbolic and with no real existence. But even if he has an inkling of it as a part of real experience he is inclined to gloss over its importance because he probably does not know what to do with it.

Yet many careful students have been led to the conclusion that a great deal of apparently psychological material is not satisfactorily explained when looked on as subjective, fantastic, and therefore unreal. It *may* be so, and the first line of analytical approach must always be to see whether the mental images of patients are not the product of their own minds. In many cases this will be so. But there will always be a residue, large or small, that cannot be accounted for in this way. On the other hand, if the principle is accepted that the mind is capable of perceiving both the thoughts of others and other phenomena not of the physical world, some at least of this residue falls into place. It may also be that physical situations are perceived by paranormal means, which add to what is learned by the senses. But these, too, need to be understood in correct terms so as to include the extra depth given by these means.

It scarcely seems necessary nowadays to offer proof that such a thing as psychic perception exists. There are many excellent books on the subject, and the reader is referred to them[1] if he wishes to study the question for himself. It is enough to say that many strict tests have been made which prove in the opinion of such men as Professor William McDougall, beyond reasonable doubt, the possibility of man extending his senses further than the range ordinarily attributed to them. People have apparently seen things happening at the other end of the world, or objects locked up in opaque boxes; they have received 'messages' and information from people miles away; they have described events in detail before they have occurred or seemed likely to occur. These and other recorded instances are so numerous and so well attested

[1] For instance, J. B. Rhine's books; J. Sinel's *The Sixth Sense*; Hereward Carrington's *Psychology in the Light of Psychic Phenomena*; *Proceedings of the Society for Psychical Research*, and many another. See Bibliography at end of this book.

that there can be little doubt about them. They seem to take place through some faculty beyond the ordinary physical senses, which makes the individual capable of perceiving objects and sounds out of the range of sight and hearing.

Broadly speaking, psychic perceptivity may be said to concern itself with two orders of objects. One—as in Zener card tests or experiments where physical objects are perceived without the use of the physical senses. The other is where non-physical and hence, to some, non-existent objects such as the state of mind of other people, or such mythical creatures as fairies or angels, are the subject of perception. Clearly, the first cases are subject to proof and even to controlled experiment, while the latter are more indefinite. To perceive the thoughts and feelings of another person, for instance, is quite a different thing from seeing that person's physical body writing at his desk, even though he be half a continent away. Nevertheless, though proof is rare, it is a commonplace experience, especially for people having close ties of affection, to be aware of one another's moods and thoughts, even though they may be out of reach of the physical senses. Careful observation will give proof that this is so; not, perhaps, as strict a proof as the most sceptical scientist will ask for, but nevertheless sufficient for the open-minded investigator.[1] Moreover, the lack of laboratory proof is probably more than made up by the universality of such experi-

[1] There is a great deal of difference between the kind of proof demanded by a laboratory worker and that which a reasonable and intelligent person is entitled to accept. The first must make his case as hermetically sealed as possible, but the second may well content himself with proof of a thing which fits in and is consistent with his own experience. The scientist must look on himself and all others as potentially 'bad witnesses'. The other can allow more laxity and within reason assume good faith.

ences. In this case, it is not a matter of the perception of physical objects, but of a different class of things, which we term psychic.

When one considers the nature of psychic objects, one has to face at once the question of what and where they are. Clearly, they cannot be weighed and measured by any means known to science. But it cannot therefore be said that they do not exist objectively and in their own right. Here we have to consider the almost universal evidence of psychically sensitive people. For though these people differ in matters of detail, they agree on the main point, which is that psychic objects have shape, size and colour, different in quality from those of physical objects yet basically the same. This immediately raises the question as to how much of the appearance of a psychic object belongs to the object itself, and how much of it is due to the contents of the mind of the person who perceives it. A correspondent, in a rather flippantly worded letter sums the situation up so neatly that it is worth quoting as he wrote it. 'The apparently real form of the psychic fact perceived by the sensitive person *may* be contributed by that person, and may therefore be subjective. I mean: an angel appears to Mrs. Higgins and tells her her son is this, that, or t'other. Had it wings and a white nightie? "Of *course* it 'ad," says Mrs. Higgins indignantly. Now, some will take the line that it was a "real" angel *because* it had white wings, etc. Others will disbelieve for the same reason, and say that Mrs. Higgins contributed the white wings. Whereas the truth would seem to be that Mrs. Higgins contributed the wings, etc., or that the visitant chose a garb in which Mrs. Higgins would recognize it for what it was. (Otherwise its visit would be wasted.) I.e. the angel was a psychic reality, but didn't necessarily have in eternity, the form under which it appeared to Mrs. Higgins.'

This comment raises three possibilities:

(a) That there are living inhabitants of the non-physical worlds; that they can alter their appearance at will; and that they have the intelligence to choose a suitable form in which to present themselves to those who see them.

(b) That our conventional representations of these psychic entities are intuitive reproductions of their appearance.

(c) That the percipient translates what he perceives into the form in which he is used to thinking of that particular kind of entity—fairy, angel, and such-like.

The matter is, however, not so simply disposed of. For, while from the physical viewpoint there are no objects apart from those in the physical world, it is not logical to assert that another form of objective life and existence is outside the possibilities of the universe. At the same time, seeing the personal element which must perforce enter into every form of direct perception, including the physical, one is entitled to ask oneself how much of actual reality there is in the descriptions of psychics, and how much is derived from their own mental conditioning.

These mental habits, and indeed, all descriptive language, are derived from the physical world, and this biases the psychic percipient towards describing what he sees in terms of this world. Moreover, preconceptions may suggest the form of an object which overclothes the reality of an object. It is evident that the personal element will be even more pronounced where psychic observation of psychic objects is concerned, by virtue of the subjective elements in the whole process of perception. The physical world has at least consistency of size, a measure of time, standards by which one object or event can be compared with another. In the psychic realm such standards can only be applied extra-sensory of objects in the physical world. But perception of psychic objects is incapable of objective measurement or comparison. Hence the possibilities of confusion are immense—and indeed it is astonishing that there is so large a measure of agreement among psychics about the things they see.

Thus, if we allow ourselves to suppose that the psychic world contains a fauna and a population of its own—a fact which cannot be proved but which is suggested by masses of experience both among sophisticated and primitive people—we can be almost certain that what the psychic describes is not a photographic image of the creature he has seen. If it is perception of an external and independent entity at all, and not merely a figment of the imagination, he will have distorted the original sense-impression, in his own mind if nowhere else.

In addition to this, psychic forms appear to be mobile and plastic, and if the entity perceived is intelligent it may add an additional distorting factor by adapting itself to what is expected by the mental cast of the person to whom it shows itself.

Consequently, when it comes to a description of psychic objects and apparitions it is impossible to be dogmatic as to their form, even though one may feel reasonably certain of their existence in any given case.

We have thus to consider the problem of the 'psychics' (to coin a word for the science of that realm equivalent to that of physics for the physical world). If the psychic world is material what kind of matter is it? And does it obey the same laws as the physical?

The first point we need scarcely consider. We are just

beginning to know something of the nature of physical matter, but we still have not the full picture of it, and it is scarcely to be expected that we can go further. But if the psychic world is material, it probably belongs to the same order as physical matter. That is, it is some kind of electro-magnetic field, though obviously on a different scale and on a different range of energy-levels. In any case, the details are unimportant from a practical angle. We know in theory that the piece of solid, tough steel girder on which perhaps our life depends is mostly 'not there' and consists mainly of intangible space, but we go on living just as when we thought it was as solid as it appears to our senses.

On the other hand, certain attributes of matter are as important in the psychic as in the physical realm. Particularly is this so in the case of those we call space and time: do these exist in the psychic world? And if so, in what form?

To these questions a tentative answer can be given: that we probably know directly something of the nature of space-time in the psychic world from the fluidity of our mental processes, our imagination, and especially from our memories of dreams. These suggest that, whereas in the physical world space and time are fixed, 'absolute' in the sense that objects keep their same relative proportions, undergo the same rhythmic changes, whether observed by man or not,[1] in the mental or psychic realm both space and time are plastic and fluidic: else the oddities of events in

[1] This is not to say that these objects are, in their own nature as man sees them. But it seems fairly certain that something exists in its own, absolute way, to which the mental image presenting in our minds has some relation. Man could be removed from this planet, and what we know as cyclic seasonal changes would still go on and affect the objects in the world just as they do now.

our minds would not be possible. Yet it would not be correct to say that space and time are already transcended. For if they were, there could be none of the sequential processes of thinking nor the spacial quality of images of objects dreamed about. Indeed, if one goes further, one can pick out rare moments of experience in which one really seems to have gone outside the realm of space-time. Here one is faced with an experience of spaceless universality, of timeless 'now-ness'. And, moreover, such moments invariably have a transformative effect on the one who undergoes them, because he realizes that he has touched a level of experience superior to and outside of the normal realm of mental and physical life—one which makes the latter seem dark, unreal, limited and even shoddy.

We may thus suggest three orders of space-time experience: that of physical, absolute or clock time (a clock being an instrument made by man for his own ends to keep himself in gear with absolute time). At the other pole is what we experience as time-space-less 'here-now-everywhere-always'. Between these is the place where absolute space-time and space-timelessness mingle, having a quality of realitive plasticity and fluidity which combines the characteristics of both extremes.

But the mingling may be said to vary in the proportions of each, according to how 'near' the perceptive centre of the individual is to either end. If it is near or at the physical, what is perceived in the psychic realm will have characteristics akin to those of physical objects. If at the opposite, they will be more abstract, general, formless, luminous. The first will be more phenomenal in meaning and value, the second more noumenal.

In short, we can speak of physical perceptivity at one end of the scale, of spiritual insight at the other, and of psychic perceptivity in between. The latter we can divide into two main types: extra-sensory perception, akin to physical sense-perception, where objects have quasi-physical form; and intuition nearer the other end, where the form is less evident, but the perception takes the form of direct knowledge, unformulated in sensory terms.

The whole scale of perceptivity will run unbroken from physical sense perception, through psychic sensitivity to spiritual illumination. The middle range partakes in varying measure of the qualities of the two extremes.

This statement needs amplification, as it concerns the 'placing' of psychic perceptivity in regard to the other functions of the mind, even though it involves a digression into theory, a useful way of doing this is to borrow the scheme suggested by Professor C. G. Jung.

It tells us that the psyche of man has four cardinal functions: thinking and feeling (emotion), sensation (physical) and intuition, two pairs having complementary qualities. Jung puts them diagrammatically thus:

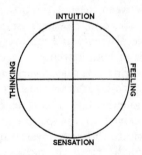

DIAGRAM 1. The Psychic Functions according to C. G. Jung.

His definition of intuition includes all the forms of perception otherwise than through the physical senses—i.e.

both psychic perception and what we have called insight.

A moment's consideration of thought and feeling will show us that these are complementary in quality but that, in practice, they are inseparable. Nobody can think, however clearly and objectively, without some modicum of feeling, nor can he feel, however passionately, without some thought to his feeling. We may thus conceive of the place from which a man thinks and feels as along a line joining the extremes of pure thought and pure feeling, the focal point indicating the proportion of thought to that of feeling at any moment. A further point emerges, that thought and feeling, no matter what they are about, are internal, subjective processes. They take place within the framework of the psychic or mental structure as one reflects on the different aspects of a situation or an object. The mind works back and forth around it and indeed a word for the joint thinking-feeling function might well be *reflection*.

The other pair of functions, however, intuition and sensation is of things outside the psyche: even spiritual insight is of things transcending the confines of the normal mind. So it seems reasonable to suggest that here, too, the point of perception may lie anywhere on an axis between physical sensation and complete insight, combining something of both extremes. And this combination of something from both would apply to all perceptions. Physical objects, perceived through the physical senses, would mean nothing without a crumb of illuminated insight, while spiritual insight and vision utterly and entirely unrelated to physical sense language would equally remain a blank.

If now we bring the two functions together, on the lines of Jung's diagram, we add something to our picture, which modifies the original thus:

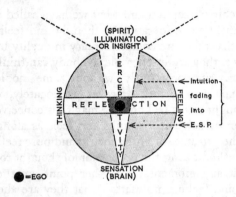

DIAGRAM 2. The circle in this diagram represents the individual mind or psyche. The lightly shaded areas represent the personal unconscious, the part outside the circle the collective. Consciousness is to all intents and purposes the dark area round the ego. The perceptive function is shown as widening out from its narrowest point, the physical brain, until it reaches the place of limitless insight, the spiritual level. The area of conscious life is shown as larger than physical consciousness alone, as experience shows that consciousness, when detached from the physical organism (see text) always appears to be much greater than that of ordinary conditions of waking life.

The result is that:

(a) A new term has been introduced, *perceptivity*, which covers the whole gamut of sensation and intuition as set out by Jung, with extremes as already suggested in insight and physical sensation.

(b) We see thought and feeling, or reflection, weaving across perceptivity. The result is consciousness, the ego, or centre of identity of the individual being at the crossing-point.

It should be added that, though in the diagram, the whole system is shown as centred and balanced, the crossing-point may at any moment be off-centre, in any direction. Thus, if there were strong feeling and little thought about a spiritual experience, the crossing-point would be in the upper right-hand quadrant, while clear thought about a physical matter would put it in the lower left-hand quadrant. In all cases, *ego* would move temporarily to the crossing-point, and thus the fabric of experience is woven, by innumerable crossings of the warp of perceptivity with the weft of reflection.

To complete the picture we should realize that it is the ex-centricity of *ego*, whether habitual or quasi-permanent, which not only prevents the balance and integration of the perfected mind, but which makes for both differences in psychological types, and that between Self and *ego*, between the spiritual and the personal nature of the individual. For *ego* is an aspect of the spiritual Self, detached and dethroned for evolutionary and experimental purposes.

In this book we are of course primarily concerned with a study of the middle field of the perceptive function, that concerned with extra-sensory, or psychic perception. If the suggestions made above are accepted, many will doubt that the power to perceive extra-sensorily, or through special psychic senses, is a widespread one. Many of the books referred to are concerned with exceptional people, or with exceptional conditions affecting ordinary people. Often, these people or conditions are unhealthy and morbid: they are in trance or drugged, emotionally overstrained, or in acute fear, ill or shocked. In these conditions startling things are perceived, but they come sporadically and in a completely erratic manner. Moreover, they are often confused with material which belongs solely to the observer's own mind and are a mixture of psychological and psychic factors. But at the other end of the scale is the work of parapsychologists. In this, tests are performed under strict laboratory control, with people in a healthy, alert state of body and mind: quite a different thing from the negative conditions of illness and hysteria. The remarkable fact is that even under the very matter-of-fact conditions of a laboratory, and in performing tests which in themselves are dull and devoid of human interest, it has been estimated that about 50 per cent of people have, or can develop, the faculties required for experiments in clairvoyance and telepathy.

In our view, however, it is probable that a very much larger proportion of people are psychically perceptive, whether they know it or not. In short, psychic perceptivity is not the property of a few but is an integral part of the mechanism of the human mind: it is as universal as sight and hearing, though often undeveloped and unconscious. It is not the property of the few, even though those possessed of developed psychic faculties often insist—and for obvious reasons—that their powers are exceptional and God-given treasures: if this were not so, it would mean admitting that they are just ordinary people. Yet in spite of the kind of cult which arises from the attempt to exalt psychic gifts by making them out to be mysterious and exceptional, there is nothing morbid and unhealthy about psychic perception. Nor is there anything unusual about it, though many people are surprised when they discover themselves to be innately and naturally psychic.

All of this may seem far-fetched. But it is a matter which lends itself to research and experiment. In research it often becomes essential to make the assumption that the thing which is to be studied may exist: only then can one start looking for it. Nothing would be known about the atom, the law of gravity, or the theory of relativity, if investigators had not had in their minds some such thought as 'I wonder whether the fact is . . . ?' With this, one can examine an idea, collect data, and see whether it holds good or not. In other words, creative research can only be done with an open mind, which is prepared to play lightly with a new idea for the purpose of finding out whether or not it is true. To start with pure negation, and to demand positive proof before even considering a theory, is the surest way of preventing oneself from obtaining that proof. Briefly, if one denies absolutely the possibility of a seam of coal existing under the ground of one's backyard and takes no steps to look and see, this is a sure way of never finding out whether or not it is there. Thus, before asserting that common psychic experience does not occur, one must, as a first step, assume that there may be such a thing.

If one then decides to set to work and investigate the matter, it is useful to have someone who can suggest methods, ask pertinent questions, criticize intelligently, and in general give a lead. This applies to any branch of research, but more especially to research about oneself or one's capacities, since in this field it is so particularly difficult to be detached and unprejudiced. Failing a teacher, co-operative work with another person in the same line has a curious way of enhancing and stimulating one's own faculties, and even if that person is no more clear and objective than oneself it is still a help in checking one's experiments. But where neither has the psychic side of himself in focus, especially if he has no psychological self-knowledge, only confused and inconclusive results are to be expected. One need only imagine two young children alone in the engineering section of South Kensington Museum: they would be completely at sea as to the meaning and purpose of the machines they saw for the first time; their speculations would be very strange and fantastic unless some adult with more expert knowledge came to their rescue.

It is in any case not an easy task to learn the technique of accurate observation. People need to be taught, not only *how* to look at a thing, but also *what* to look for. This needs long and arduous training, repeated experiments and, above all, that one should not be deterred when one has made a mistake.

In all probability the first thing to be discovered is that the physical senses are often a source of information which might be thought to be psychically perceived. Subtle changes of expression, slight changes of tension and posture, are physical phenomena, often scarcely describable, yet they often serve as a lead to knowing that a person's mood has changed. But, more than this, they often serve as a channel to deeper knowledge of the other person than the surface change alone. In other words, they can be the starting point from which the observer enters the field of psychic perceptivity, which is none the less genuine for having been started from the physical end.

There is, moreover, a considerable overlapping between the physical and psychic levels. There is, as it were, a region of twilight between them, just as there is a period where day and night overlap and one fades into the other. Some people are at times very much aware of this half-way state, in which they are conscious of using their ordinary physical senses, but with something added which changes the values of their perceptive power. It is as though they stood between two worlds and were able to observe simultaneously two aspects of the same thing. Yet the relationship between the perceiving self and the world it is perceiving is the same.

In the physical realm we recognize the world outside as

having its own life and existence. Rivers flow, the sun rises and sets, the wind blows, without reference to us. We can observe this world, register what it shows us, and, when we know how, can produce changes in it by action. The relationship between the physiological and the external physical world is so familiar that it need not be stressed.

Considered from this angle, the psychological world is inside ourselves. It is a compound of personal feelings and memories: at the same time, it is sequential, though the sequence may not be immediately obvious; and, if we analyse deeply enough, every part is in some way linked with the rest by associations of thought and feeling, making up a whole—though not always a tidy, well-shaped whole.

The psychic world, however, is like the physical in that what is observed can be entirely independent of us. It does not originate in our own history or memory, our likes or dislikes, but has a spontaneous life and activity of its own. Moreover, what we see of it may be, and often is, quite unrelated to ourselves. It is impersonal. In the present stage of our development it appears erratic and ungovernable, but as we can observe the physical world through the physical senses so we can learn to observe the psychic world by using our psychic or extra-sense; and, if we learn how, we can produce changes in it, just as we can produce changes in the material world. This is called magic; for real magic is but the active or willed aspect of psychic activity, just as our action in the physical world is the active side of physical functions.

The overlap between the psychic and physical perception is particularly clear when one comes to study the nature of what is perceived by the psychic senses. As we have said, two main classes of objects perceived by them become evident:

PSYCHIC AND PSYCHOLOGICAL

1. Physical objects seen in a way in which the physical senses cannot see them. Thus, it is possible to see an object enclosed in an opaque box, a stone in a kidney, to read an unopened letter, to see or hear things taking place at the other end of the world.

2. Psychic objects, which do not exist concretely in the physical world: such things as the thoughts and emotions of other people, the past or future history of events in certain places, and such-like. These form a subdivision of this class, and they associate with physical occurrences or with human activity.

Psychic objects and beings not related to physical objects or produced by the mind of the percipient himself form a mysterious subdivision of the second order of psychic observations. They appear to exist *per se* in the psychic world, as fish do in the sea. They often seem to live their life according to laws pertaining to their own nature and to that of their world, just as other creatures live in the physical world.

But are they in reality as we perceive them? As in the case of Mrs. Higgins's angel, the answer is, probably not. In the physical world our minds produce an image which is related to the actual object. But, as presented to the mind of the observer—like the steel bar already mentioned—the picture is conditioned by the limitations of the senses. How much more must this be so when the mind looks at creatures and things made of 'such stuff as dreams are made of'—i.e. mind-stuff? Not only does the object itself appear to be fluid and plastic, in form, but, in addition, we must always remember that the perceiving mind is rarely clear and unbiased.

Hence, on theoretical grounds, it is most unlikely that a ghost, an angel, or any other psychic entity exists in its own right in the form in which it is psychically perceived.

PSYCHIC AND PSYCHOLOGICAL

Under the circumstances, it is surprising that there is so great a consensus of agreement as to the shape of such beings as angels, *devas*, demons and the like. The reason probably is dual: on the one hand, that the forms are archetypal to man; that is, they are part of the common mental heritage of mankind, so that a Chinese, an Indian or a European will relate the same basic form to a given psychic entity, while varying details according to race and tribe. The other may be that the archetypal form (quasi-human in the case of angels or *devas*) belongs to some fundamental pattern in the universe. If so, all creatures of the universal Mind—whether we call this God or by the modern name of Natural Law—exist in the basic form of all beings living within the field of that Mind.

The real solution to the problem can, however, only come, first as the psychic improves his technique and learns to use his powers of observation objectively, then when he reaches the further end of the perceptive range, and begins to see things as they *are*, not only as they *appear*. Most people are still in the stage where they do not know the frontiers of their own mind, where to draw the line between their own thoughts and ideas and those of others. Still less can they be objective in determining what are the contents of this mind and what are the things outside it and existing on their own account in the external psychic worlds. Only training and analysis can clarify the situation; and this training in clear psychic perception must be linked with training in psychological technique: to know the world outside oneself one must know th world inside oneself, also. The converse is equally true.

The following story[1] is one which illustrates clearly the

[1] This kind of experience, as well as others which will be found in the text, needs documentation and the corroborative evidence of others in order to be acceptable to scientific psychical research workers. The purpose

objectivity of a purely psychic experience. It is one which, by its very nature, cannot be confused with psychological experience—i.e. processes taking place within the mind of the observer and having a meaning and value personal to himself. It is related by a friend who was a natural-born psychic and took psychic visits for granted, as a part of her everyday life. It is a characteristic psychic episode, because it has no relationship to any previous experience, or to any desire of the percipient, and was as casual as if one were accosted by a stranger in the street.

'I was staying with friends, and one night about 1 a.m. I was beginning to feel drowsy when I became aware of someone in the room. I knew it was not a person in a physical body, but a very live and innocent "ghost". I had the impression he was blundering about because the room was strange. At first I was too drowsy to bother, but the blundering went on, until at last, in a fit of irritation, I sat upright in bed to see what was happening. In the middle of the room stood a dark man, young, alert, dressed as an airman. I particularly noticed the way his hair grew, and various personal things about him, notably that he had only one arm, and the artificial arm ended in an old-fashioned hook.

'Then I said crisply, feeling by this time rather cross,

of this book, however, is not to offer proved cases: this can be, and is, far better done elsewhere. Nevertheless, the cases given—even should they be decidedly 'not proven'—can serve another purpose, which is to illustrate certain types of events and the principles underlying them. The latter is the purpose of this book, rather than to add yet another to the many excellent volumes already extant where watertight cases of psychic happenings are to be found. In fact, if the validity of the experiences described is challenged, and other interpretations are offered, the answer to the challenger would be to say that, on the evidence given in these very books, the onus might well be put on him to prove that these experiences were *not* of that order we call psychic.

"What do you want?" In a quick, imperative voice he shot out, "Tell my wife . . .", then gave several clear business instructions, and ended up by saying, "Tell her I am doing my damnedest for her and the kids." Then, in a flash, he was gone.

'I realized at once that he was an absolute stranger. I had no idea of his name, where he came from, nor anything about his wife; so I promptly lay down, consigned him to oblivion, and went to sleep.

'Next morning I told my hostess, and completely forgot the whole incident. Three or four weeks later my telephone bell rang to summon me to go to visit a stranger. As I sat talking to her, my glance wandered round the room. With a start of surprise I saw on the mantelpiece a large head-and-shoulders photograph of the man I had seen in my room three weeks before. This time he was dressed in ordinary clothes, but the likeness was indisputable. The artificial arm was not visible. She was pouring out a stream of rather hysterical talk, as many badly shocked people do, when I broke in:

' "Forgive me, but I must take a risk in talking to you in an unconventional way. Have you, by any chance, just lost your husband, and did he die in an air crash?"

'She sat upright with a jerk, and exclaimed, "Yes! But how did you know?"

'I said, "I did not know until I came into this room. Is this a good likeness of your husband?"

'Then, in minute detail, I gave her a description of the husband, his voice, his curious manner of shooting out words, like shots out of a gun, and ended by saying, "There is one acid test which either puts this into court or throws it out completely." Then I told her about the artificial arm.

'At that she went deathly white, and said, "That proves

it. He lost his arm in the war but was such a keen airman that nothing could keep him out of the air, so a special machine was made in which he could use an iron hook instead of his hand."

'I then gave her the business instructions and the end of his message, at which a look of relief came over her face and she replied, "I have been worried to death about finance, and the children, and the last part of his message is exactly what he would have said."

'The story was that the man was engaged in civil flying, and had crashed, leaving his affairs in a muddle. It was obviously his job to try and do something about it, which he did by using me as a sort of telephone.'

The experience just related is unusual on two counts. First, because of its rather dramatic nature: and second, because it was significant to a person other than the one concerned in the actual psychic experience. As a rule, these things are of no importance or value to anybody but the person who experiences them. In this case the transmitter, having been consciously psychic all her life, had taken the experience itself as an everyday thing and did not see anything unusual in it until she saw the photograph. A third point is that it appeared to anticipate certain events and arrangements which had not yet been considered. This, however, is not unusual, because some part of us does appear to be able to look ahead and around corners, at any rate at times. Dunne, in his book *An Experiment with Time*, discusses precognition at length, and there are many other recorded instances.[1]

The example is an unusually convincing one to illustrate what we mean when we say that psychic—as distinct from psychological—experience is quite impersonal and detached from ourselves. The message had no more to do

[1] See, for instance, the *Proceedings of the Society for Psychical Research*.

with the transmitter than the letter a postman delivers has to do with him; nor did the airman and his widow have anything personal to do with the psychic who did them the service.

In other cases the detached nature of what is perceived is much less obvious, because it is so difficult altogether to eliminate the unconscious mind. This has a well-known way of playing tricks by making us believe that things are outside our mind when, in reality, they are inside it. The result is delusions, hallucinations, indeed nine-tenths of what the untrained observer believes to be psychic material. The common fault among people who have slight psychic ability is to attribute far more to the super-normal than is actually the case. The following experience, is typical.

'On a gloomy November afternoon, just before dark, I was waiting for my husband, and amused myself by watching the market square and trying to pick out from the dim silhouetted figures which flitted across it, the differing figures of men and women. I wondered idly if I could recognize my husband's in the heavy dusk. It was far too dark to distinguish the difference between a man in his overcoat and a woman in a short frock: the figures were just moving black shadows. Suddenly, emerging from the far side of the square, a shadow moved forward, and I knew it was my husband. There was no possibility of see-ing him, but I instantly recognized him by his alert charac-teristic movements, and I smiled to myself because I thought of a certain friend who, with great gusto, would have announced, "I knew John psychically," or "I knew it was John by his aura."'

Here are some others which serve to show how the people concerned got their first glimpse of the objective psychic world.

The first is an account given by a medical psychologist. 'I was treating a patient, a young woman, with whom, had I met her socially, I should have had very little in common. I mention this because the fact that she was not a person in whom I would have any personal interest, makes the experience more arresting. She lay on a couch while she talked. I could see neither her face nor her expression. One day as she talked, quietly and apparently calmly, I found myself becoming frightened. I asked myself "Why?" The patient belonged to a non-conformist chapel which she attended regularly, and she was talking about a sermon full of hell-fire and the like. I asked myself whether by any chance she had stirred up in me a latent fear of these doctrines. I have never had anything to do with chapels, and I was not brought up in any of the crude ideas of hell and damnation, so I felt this was not the cause of my fear. Casting around in my mind for the reason, I hit on the idea that the fear was not mine but the patient's, which I had absorbed into myself, and thought I was generating. I therefore said quietly, "Why are you so frightened?" Whereupon the patient gave a start, and said, "Goodness, so I am! But I did not realize it until you spoke. How did you know?"

'I came to the conclusion that I had actually picked up psychically an emotion which was not mine but somebody else's. I had identified myself with it, or it with me, and momentarily thought it was my own. This experience opened my eyes to the possibility of such happenings, and I was able on many occasions to verify the same phenomenon. Moreover, and this is important, I discovered that as soon as I recognized that the feeling was not my own, but an external influence invading the privacy of my psyche, I no longer felt the emotion in question. It was as if analysis and examination shut a window, so that I was able to look out and say, "The wind is blowing," but there was no longer a draught in the room of my own personality.'

This case brings out two interesting points. First, it shows the ease with which the doctor was invaded by an outside atmosphere created by someone else. Secondly, it illustrates the principle that immunity can be secured by a mental withdrawal from such a situation and by a critical examination of it.

Another instance is of a woman in her thirties, in excellent physical health. She was referred to a psychologist for treatment because she had frequent attacks of sickness and digestive disturbance for which there was no physical reason. Psychotheraphy revealed a difficult childhood, leading on to a marriage with a man of strong emotions, unbalanced and feckless in his ways. The patient herself was of a sensitive type, with a character devoid of clear focus and determination, who let herself be dominated by her husband, her parents, or anyone stronger than herself.

Much of her psychological material was analysed out, and her relations with others became clear to her, showing her where, at times, loyalties conflicted. It was, however, not at these crises that she had her attacks. It became increasingly apparent that they occurred when she had been in the presence of some strong, disruptive emotion, such as a fit of anger in her husband. Further investigation showed the patient to be highly sensitive to atmosphere and psychic situations. In fact, part of her apparent weakness of character was due to the fact that she was defenceless against the feelings of others, for these flowed straight into her before she was aware of them. She learned to regard her problem as largely psychic, and one day arrived in the consulting-room jubilant with her first success in defending herself against psychic onslaught. She had been writing at her desk, and suddenly felt 'all gone' at the pit of the stomach, rapidly becoming depressed. On this occasion she had pulled herself together and looked for the cause. She eliminated what she was writing; there was nothing there to depress. The weather was fine. She had no particular fear or worry in her mind. Then she chanced on the idea, 'It is not I, it is Jim.' The moody husband was correcting proofs in the same room, and within a few minutes he remarked, 'I am fed up!' flung down his proofs, and walked out of the room, slamming the door. This showed the patient *for herself*, in a way no amount of theoretical exposition could have done, how much she was psychically open and in need of re-education if she was to learn to protect herself. Being a woman of intelligence, she gradually learned how to handle her psychic temperament positively, and so to avoid the crises of sickness. It is clear that, no matter how much more psychological analysis and readjustment she might have had, it would have failed to deal with her psychic over-receptivity. The psychological work cleared the field and brought her basic problem to the surface. It failed to deal with it, for it had to be tackled from a different angle. When she realized the influence of objective psychic facts upon her over-receptive psychic nature, she became aware of what actually happened and dealt with it as a real situation, just as she had learned to deal with her subjective psychological conditions when revealed to her through psychotheraphy. Like the physician in the last case she found that half the battle was won by knowing this.

Here is another example of direct psychic perception.

'One day a doctor walked into my room saying that he had been introduced by another doctor who was a mutual friend. He wished to discuss psychic matters and particularly to find out what his own powers were and how he could use them to the best advantage in his practice.

'We talked for a little and I found him exceptionally argumentative. I was busy, and did not want to waste further time and effort, so I said, abruptly, "Dr. ——, you did not come here to discuss these matters at all. You are not really interested."

'He replied, "What did I come for?"

'In rather an exasperated mood, I said, "You came to find out if the woman you are in love with will get her divorce, and whether you will be able to marry her. You are sailing abroad to-morrow; and you have no intention of taking trouble to develop your own latent faculties."

'At that he threw back his head and laughed and admitted that this was so.

'We parted quite amicably.'

This example, again, is one in which no ordinary psychological explanation will fit. It is a straightforward illustration of extra-sensory or psychic perception.

In this case the ostensible purpose of the visit was merely camouflage. Under it lay curiosity as to the capacities of the psychic. But the dominant preoccupation of the doctor's mind was with a personal problem strongly coloured by emotion. This registered as the true object of the visit and was the strongest mental current of the three. Consequently, it was picked up by the psychic, in spite of the attempts to conceal it under small talk.

This last illustration is taken from the experience of an individual who has always been psychically self-conscious. It is chosen because it is clear of entanglement with the psychological field. The other two, though less detached, are typical of what may occur to any psychically sensitive person.

It is only fair to add a warning at this point. To be markedly psychically perceptive is not to lie on a bed of roses—or, if the richness of life unfolded by this sensitivity seems to make it a road of 'roses, roses all the way', it will be found that roses have thorns. These thorns are that the psychic is like a highly sensitized and carefully balanced instrument, subjected to all the jolts and collisions which a world oblivious of fine feelings must give to such a person. If one is already, by nature, such a sensitive instrument, there is no remedy for it. But if the delicate mechanism is working all the time, and recording both pleasant and unpleasant things in the dark, it is surely better to learn to know this in full consciousness, rather than be the victim of its insidious workings deep in the unconscious foundations of the mind. In so far, therefore, as it is a danger and makes life more difficult for one, it is better to have that danger in sight, so that one can know what it is doing or likely to do, and so take steps to counter its assault on one's contentment.

Yet, as we have pointed out, psychic perceptivity, consciously understood or controlled, more than sets off the unpleasant shocks we get from it, because it gives us a deeper perspective on life in all its aspects. Psychism is not a thing to dabble in, any more than it is wise to dabble in psychology, or any other science. Nor is it safe to try and open up, prematurely, faculties which are not already open. But it *is* wise to seek out and learn to know and use intelligently such faculties as already exist and are active in the personality, especially when they are apt to become troublesome through neglect and lack of proper control and discipline.

CHAPTER III

Historical

The historical approach to a subject is often tedious. But it is necessary, in order to understand our subject, to have a thread of continuity. Otherwise, the relationship between the various stages of perception is not seen. Each stage represents a logical development from the preceding one and, consequently, contains within it the characteristics of its predecessors. It follows that, to grasp the significance of the present-day structure of the mind, one must know something of the background out of which it has grown. Moreover, this history needs to be correlated with the phases of psychic perception at various periods of its development, as well as with the instinctive life of animals. Further, there appears to be a correspondence which is of primary importance between these things and the evolution of the central nervous system.

Psychological medicine states that mental troubles and difficulties result in a tendency to regress from the stage of mental and emotional development one has reached, or should have reached, to one more primitive. Or—to say the same thing from a different angle—difficulties arise from a failure to keep up to date with oneself. It is clearly a possible source of trouble if the mind of a person remains infantile and his body is adult, or if the emotions are those of a child and the intellect has gone ahead to the elaboration and skill of a trained scientist. If this principle is applied, as indeed it must be, to men's psychic experience, it will be necessary to understand not only the evolution

71

of the psychic faculties, but also the reason of their neglect and consequent immaturity at present. Only then shall we be able to estimate their true place in adult psychological life. This immaturity is far more common than is usually realized, since modern education has so far tackled only the psychological development of the child and leaves the psychic faculties untouched. These frequently remain in an infantile condition, trying and failing to keep up with their adult and well-grown sister.

Man, it is often said, is an animal. Some people go no further because to do so takes them into metaphysical difficulties, and, further, imposes on them inconvenient ethical and moral restrictions. Others, agreeing, add that he is an animal with something added which makes him human. Some pertinently if tritely add a third point, which is that he has not yet reached the perfection of humanity—in spite of calling himself *homo sapiens*.

Man is animal: he has in him the fullness of the psychological life of the animal, which is directed by instinct. The richer the instinctive life, the better the animal. But instinct is not the private property of one animal. It is the common heritage of all. It is a vast ocean of urge to live, to procreate, to perpetuate the species. Within it arise currents by which one variety of animal becomes in some particular different from another. But there is nothing individual about instinct: it is collective, and the single animal, be he never so domestic and sophisticated, must conform to the collective type. He cannot be said to exist as an individual, or to know himself as one. There is no first person singular about him.

The primitive[1] or instinctive type of reaction to things about one tends to be 'all-or-none', in the sense that when

---

[1] The technical terms for 'all-or-none' primitive reactions is *protopathic*. Out of these emerge increasingly elaborate *epicritic* reactions.

one sees a frightened animal, such as a hare in her form, lying absolutely still one moment but the next in headlong flight, there are no gradations from one to the other. The reaction of the savage and of the civilized man when his civilization breaks down under great stress approximates to this level. This type of reaction changes gradually to one involving judgment and gradation. To say, 'I hear sound' or 'I hear nothing', is primitive. To say, 'I hear music: violins and wood-wind, and they are playing Beethoven' and 'This is a little less loud than that' is an elaboration of the simple fact of primitive hearing and involves the capacity to appreciate fine distinctions. There is, however, no sharp dividing line between the two, and progress shows a gradual refinement of the first into more and more finely balanced judgments as regards both perception and action. The determining force in this is the growing intellect, which, by its very nature, makes a space between the individual consciousness and the thing it is looking at, so that the object can be clearly seen. Gradually perception is sharpened until subtle shades of difference, hitherto unnoticed, come into view.

In the human sphere, the crudest instincts show themselves in mass behaviour, in mob action such as panic or anger, where rational thinking is swept away and intelligent people find themselves acting in a manner which, subsequently, surprises and horrifies them. It is plain that these urges do not operate through the ordinary range of the physical senses, but that they touch off something which is at once extra-sensory and collective, not individual. On the other hand, a strictly civilized, rational man may find himself standing aside from such surges of group feeling, able to observe them but unaffected by them; or, if affected, he is able to control his reaction to them by knowing what they are and whence they come.

HISTORICAL

The primitive person who lacks such discriminative perception is not self-contained. He is at the mercy not only of tribal—i.e. collective—law but of the forces of nature and has to propitiate them and pay for his right to life and happiness. This, among other things, makes him a slave to the magician-priest, whether this be a modern dictator or the black-robed priest of a village in a peat bog.

The power of magic over the primitive is well known, while civilized man is relatively immune. His immunity is probably due to the fact that he scoffs at it. This makes him positive enough to be unaffected by what he considers to be mere superstition; but it does not mean that magic is in itself ineffective. In fact, a study of primitive peoples shows quite the reverse, as far as they themselves are concerned. It undoubtedly works partly by suggestion. But our incipient knowledge of psycho-kinesis suggests that the magician may actually use this power in a positive way, thereby reinforcing the suggestion. It does not touch civilized man because his mind rejects it, not necessarily because it is pure illusion. An arrow is ineffective against an armoured car. But that does not mean that arrows do not exist. The ability to think supplies the armour-plate against which the bow and arrow of primitive magic is useless. Naomi Mitchison's *The Spring Queen and the Corn King* exemplifies the subservience of the savage to magic, and the freedom of the sophisticated from it. Her hero, the half-Greek, half-Scythian king of a primitive village, finds himself in dire physical danger, caught and paralysed by the sorcery of his wife. A Greek philosopher who is watching senses the danger, runs to the king, appeals to all that is Greek in him and liberates him from the spell by making him assert himself as a detached, free-thinking individual.

In the beginning, man is open indiscriminately to all

the psychic influences about him, and this includes all the forces of nature which dictate instinctive and therefore automatic patterns of behaviour. Whether any given individual is consciously aware of such psychic impacts depends on how far he has developed the sense of independent 'I-ness', on how far he is a thinking creature. Otherwise, he simply drifts in their current, following blindly whatever instinct decrees.

Instinctive behaviour follows the mandate of impersonal nature without any conscious awareness of that mandate. The gathering of swallows in the autumn, or the strange compulsion which makes thousands of lemmings rush to self-destruction by drowning, are examples of instinctive and automatic mass-behaviour. There is no evidence to suggest that the individual bird or beast has any conscious awareness of what he is doing. Human beings sometimes act in a similar automatic manner. The beginnings of discriminative perception occur when the individual realizes consciously that a demand is being made, and is able to decide whether or not he will accede to its behest.

Perceptivity arises out of the impact of instinct on something in us which offers sufficient resistance to it for us to feel it. When our senses are aroused, we get our bearings. But when they are not, we are helpless and unconscious. The simile suggests itself that instinctive behaviour is like that of a man in a boat out of sight of land. He is carried by every tide and current, and does not know it. The sight of land, however, gives him a fixed point by which he can perceive for himself that he is moving, even though he may still be unable to control the movement. Perception begins when the intellect develops enough to become separate and distinct from the sea of instinctive urges. These urges, in part at least, are external, objective; for example, those of seasonal and lunar changes, and the impulses which anticipate events, such as an unusually hard winter, months before they occur.

Some time in the process of mental evolution, the first person singular is born. As a corollary to this comes the idea of other persons and things—not-I as against I. This capacity to differentiate himself from his environment marks the real difference between animal and man. Henceforth, for many centuries, man struggles to strengthen his sense of I-ness, to differentiate himself more and more from the inchoate herd, to become an individual. Yet he carries with him that which is at once a treasure and a burden: the undifferentiated and instinctive life. It is treasure in so far as it guides his infant steps and helps him to survive the difficulties and dangers which then surround him. It becomes a millstone round his neck when, as he struggles to become an individual, he makes the mistake of trying to cut himself free from it, instead of adapting the instinctive energy to his new conception of individual life and making it serve as a means to carry him towards his superhuman goal.

The birth of the sense of selfhood takes place with the emergence of the conscious intellect, as distinct from the feeling or emotional side of the mind. In one sense it is at this point that man begins to view life as a scientist. To be scientific means to be separate from what one is studying. Emotion must not be allowed to cloud the picture; one has to be detached, impartial, and clear-cut. The need is to focus attention ever more clearly upon the subject to be considered. To focus means, in effect, to narrow one's field in order to enlarge small details which would otherwise be lost, and it is frequently necessary to study one aspect only of a subject and to eliminate any other. Clearly, man loses much at the stage where:

A primrose by the river's brim
A dicotyledon was to him,
And it was nothing more.

He loses the aesthetic value of the primrose. Yet the loss caused by focusing on a purely scientific attitude is only temporary, and if one takes a long view, more apparent than real. For, in the main, and in spite of the horrors to which the misuse of intellect now submits us, man has gained vastly by the growth of the scientific approach. He is more alert and less somnolent than he was only a century ago. Step by step, squalor, disease, and ignorance are being dealt with, and even the less successful members of the community enjoy a standard of life incomparably better than they did a few decades since. Paradoxically, the necessary narrowing of the original field has actually resulted in a widening of it for the many instruments devised to extend the range of the senses has so much enlarged the scope of things we can see directly and for ourselves.

Naturally, however, the beginner in using critical methods is not sure of himself. He therefore wants to brush aside the vague, the intangible, that which cannot be measured with some instrument. One can never be quite sure of one's own senses, but an impersonal instrument such as a ruler gives one a fixed standard by which to measure and compare, and therefore a certain sense of security in one's researches. Thus, scientists for a long time disregarded the mental functions, and psychology is a comparatively new branch of science; and even this has had to make its way through a somewhat arid field of laboratory experiment before it dared to study introspective experience and give this its necessary and proper place. Even here there is a tendency for many to limit themselves to the point of view of Freudian psychoanalysis, on the ground that it is so much more objective than that of other schools. This is because the emphasis on the physical body and its members tells us about things we know and can see, and gives at least an appearance of objectivity to the writings of this school, which some others have not got.

All this applies with even increased force to the psychic aspect of life, not only because it is still more nebulous to most people than the psychological, but because of its menace: the menace of its association with primitive mass instinct, which weighs everybody down, including the scientist himself. It is only now that the latter, after consolidating himself in some measure in his method, and after making his intellect at least partly objective and detached, can begin to consider psychic questions analytically; though he is still afraid of letting the matter come near enough to see it as an integral part of his own make-up. As already pointed out, at one time the attitude of many scientists to psychic experience was simply one of negation. Now, most of them have reached the stage of admitting that psychic perception exists, but they still keep it segregated behind intellectual bars, where it can only be examined through instruments and by an elaborate technique and without close personal contact.

This attitude is by no means illegitimate: it gives a chance for the intellect to grow and become strong to face the whole of the strange unknown. Man needs a strong, critical, analytical intellect. It is a valuable asset, even though it can be dangerously misused. Its evolutionary value is that it strengthens the individual and helps to separate him from the primitive mass. It helps him to conquer superstition and animism, to think for himself, to make his own independent judgments.

So far, therefore, the refusal of the scientific thinker—

and if we are not too strict in our definition, his number is legion—to consider psychic matters, has had a definite evolutionary value. But it is unsound that any part of the human equipment should be permanently neglected. On the contrary, to make man whole it must eventually be brought into play, enhanced and strengthened by partnership with the new mental equipment which has been gained while it was eclipsed. Evolution is a spiral in which history repeats itself. Yet there is a difference in each repetition, because with each recurring cycle human faculties move up one step, and the relation between man and his environment is altered by the introduction of new capacities. In our cycle the moment seems to have arrived for western man to make conscious his psychic life and to become aware of a side of his make-up to which his reactions have hitherto been purely unconscious and instinctive.

In the East, where mental development has been on a different line, more metaphysical than that of western science, the tradition is unbroken, and the psychic nature of man has always been included in systems of training and education. This has given a far more continuous and balanced development than the average westerner has. In the world of to-day we are beginning to see that the urgent need, without which civilization cannot survive, is to unite the very valuable practical side of western life with the deep insight into human nature of the best eastern tradition.

The mental growth of the typical westerner has led to a stage of wilful—but not malicious—blindness as far as psychic matters are concerned. This does not mean that psychic functions ceased working, but that they are as far as possible ignored and not allowed to interfere with our thought processes. At least, that is the intention, though in practice they still have a way of cropping up at inconvenient moments and upsetting carefully arranged thought.

The evolution of the psychic sense from primitive or negative into developed positive levels can best be illustrated by analogy. The savage lives in a cave or hut where one opening serves as door, window and chimney. Every wind in the forest drifts through it, swirls the smoke around the dwelling and blows things about. The next stage is to make separate openings. These still remain open to every breeze, though one may be able to determine whether the wind comes in more from one direction than another. The scientist then invents curtains and shutters, and the other world is shut out. One day he learns to combine the snug self-containedness of his personal home with letting in light and air at will, by using window glass. He can also look through the glass and observe the world outside. This last stage corresponds with the development of controlled and positive psychism which should go hand in hand with intelligent, positive thinking. With one step further, man goes even beyond this level of observation and adapts plain glass into lenses for microscopes and telescopes, which open up special fields of investigation. This corresponds to the special ability of the well-trained psychic, which can be used for exceptional purposes, such as very close and detailed study of small objects. But such advances are for the specialist rather than for the ordinary person whose task does not involve the need for what are in effect laboratory methods and appliances.

The history of the race is epitomized in every one of us. Psychologists recognize that the baby, from his birth on, recapitulates in broad outline the cultural stages of the past. He is at first primitive and purely instinctive in his reactions: all-asleep, all-pleased, all-angry. Later, he passes to more graduated steps. One day the sense of I-ness is born. Sometimes this is marked by such a change as from 'Michael wants pudding' to 'I want pudding'. Occasionally the change takes on a conscious and dramatic form such as the following: 'I was, I am sure, not more than five, when, during a walk, I quite suddenly saw my small brother, my nurse, a dog, as people quite separate from myself—living, breathing, moving independently of my will. It was a startling discovery. I was I, they were they and not myself at all. About the same time I remember thinking to myself, "There is the Moon. It looks like ... well, the Moon. But these other people may see something quite different from what I see, though they give it the same name." A curiously philosophical thought for a small boy!'

In psychic development the stages are the same. Psychologists have frequently commented on the identity of the child with the mind of its mother, as revealed in deep analysis of the early days of life, as well as in the child's own dreams, where problems are seen which are obviously not those of a child but an adult, and sometimes of a person of the opposite sex. There seems to be no barrier between the two minds, and every change of feeling and attitude of mind in the parent produces a change in the child. Under certain conditions this results in anxiety in the child, or in a feeling of insecurity, and incidentally provides an explanation as to why a child often feels happier in the care of a placid, cow-like nanny than with a brilliant but capricious mother.

A mother who understood this fact of psychic unity was very careful not to make a psychic break with her baby son. From the time he was about nine months old she made a habit of telling him when she was going out and where she was going. Though quite aware of the intellectual absurdity of this, she maintained that it somehow gave the child psychic security, and he certainly grew up stable and unafraid. In contrast to this, another mother had the unwise habit of getting her child occupied and then slipping out without his noticing she had gone. Years later, one of the grievances the child brought up against her was this repeated breaking of psychic contact. This explained to the parents much of the difficulty they had with the boy, particularly his acute attacks of temper and fear, for which there did not seem to be any ordinary psychological reason.

Naturally, the child is most affected by those closest to him, but he is psychically open to any influence within reach. One tiny boy for several years was always profoundly disturbed around about Armistice Day. Nobody in the house had any personal reason for feeling unduly strongly about it and he was far too young to understand what the celebration meant. Nevertheless, he had bad nights, with crying fits quite unaccountable except on the ground of the general atmosphere which, for many years after 1918, was one strongly charged with thoughts and feelings of regret, and of remembrance of horrible things. After two or three years, as he became physically active, vigorous and busy, this behaviour disappeared. It may well have been due to the fact that at first he was in the state of the cave-dweller with unshuttered openings to his personality, and for some reason was particularly responsive to the atmosphere of Armistice Day. Only by degrees did he begin to shut himself away and to make a self-contained home of his own. He unconsciously built his psychic walls as he began to react to things about him and to think for himself. As his individuality emerged it gave him a fixed point outside the psychic ocean, and he was able to develop himself according to his own innate pat-

HISTORICAL

tern without psychic interference from his environment.

As he grows up, the child is in any case inclined to close the doors of psychic perception. His schooling and general education emphasize the importance of material things, and the experience of these fills his mind, so that his psychic temperament becomes overlaid by thought and feeling about the physical world. In this way his more subtle reactions are often lost. But a lost thing does not cease to exist; in the psychological unconscious, where it is not allowed to develop, it naturally grows backwards towards a more primitive level of activity which is in direct contrast to the forward movement of the conscious mental life. Moreover, this primitive psychic faculty is often stirred into activity, and this at times complicates problems and the making of decisions by introducing obscure influences which cloud and confuse judgment. The psychic nature at this stage is like sediment in a glass of water: it drops to the bottom, leaving a clear, transparent conscious field; anything which disturbs the water, however, brings it up again and makes the water cloudy. This is similar to psychological associations, but it is far subtler.

Our race is, therefore, at a stage where, in order to obtain clarity and objectivity of thought it has instinctively tried to lose and forget its psychic nature. By doing this it may have won what it sought as regards purely physical things. Paradoxically, it has also frustrated itself where finer shades of perception are concerned. For while psychic perceptions may introduce subtle elements which befog the brilliance of lucid intellectual thought, these same elements enrich experience like overtones in music, and life is the poorer without them.

If we recognize and understand these factors, as well as the reasons why we ignore them and learn what can be done with them, they can be brought into their right place and fitted into the whole pattern of life. In short, it is necessary to learn to deal with the psychic faculties as an integral part of consciousness. They are normal, healthy and natural assets to acute judgment when properly handled, although they may remain as liabilities if ignored.

To-day most of us are in the intermediate stage of psychic development, where we have no clear ideas of what to do or how to do it. Even the comparatively well-trained psychic seems to have his weak points. It would appear that our race as a whole has reached a cyclic turn and has just stepped over the threshold of a new period when this aspect of human experience once more needs to be included and accepted in everyday life. This is borne out by the general acceptance of people with psychic gifts. Few people are without acquaintance with someone who has a flair for telling fortunes or who has some form of second sight. People so gifted are no longer shunned as abnormal or considered to be necessarily charlatans and frauds. On the contrary, there is a great deal of interest shown in them, and they are usually very popular in their immediate circle. What is not realized is that some faculty of like kind exists somewhere in each member of that circle as well as in those outside it. Nor does popular interest include any serious study of the rationale of what is taking place, since people are usually more interested in sensational happenings than in finding out why and how they happen.

CHAPTER IV

Mechanism—I

The Psycho-Physical Bridge

The body, with its many organs, enables us to perceive and to act on the material world around us. The range of perception and activity depends upon the health and capacity of the body. The blind, the deaf, and the lame show us the limitations imposed upon personal experience when part of the physical mechanism is deficient. The same principle applies to psychic activity. Like the physical, it must have a healthy and complete mechanism in order to express itself adequately at its own level.

The physical mechanism is known in detail. Its study may be laborious, but it is not difficult. For one thing, it has special extension and a form which is comparatively fixed. Only the physical senses, even if their range is extended by the use of apparatus, are needed. It is otherwise with the psychic organism, because of its fluidity, the lability of its forms, the rapidity of its movement. No physical instrument, however delicate and sensitive, could keep pace with it even were it able to register its existence. The student of it has, hence, to fall back on subjective impressions on the one hand, or on extra-sensory perception on the other, if he wishes to understand it.

The first is valid. But there is difficulty in studying anything when one is using that thing both as the object of study and the means of studying it. So self-examination, valuable as it is in many ways, cannot tell us much about the structure of the psyche. Clairvoyance or some other form of e.s.p., however, is the only other means at our disposal.

There are very few who have the clairvoyant faculty sufficiently developed and well-focused to be able to study it directly.

Trained clairvoyants have made many investigations and have recorded their results. These explain and make clear the cryptic accounts in certain ancient mystical and occult books, and it is found that these direct observations largely dovetail with the descriptions given in the old traditions.

Materialistic psychology and physiology equate brain and mind. This might be so, except that overwhelming evidence has been accumulated to show that, while the brain and nervous system are the physical seat of the psyche, the psyche can nevertheless experience the sensations of leaving that seat and function apart from it. 'I' am capable of feeling and thinking while the body is unconscious, and there are many recorded instances where people have watched their unconscious bodies from outside and found themselves complete in regard to all aspects of feeling and thinking, and have been able to make their observations of the inert physical form. The following cases illustrate this. In all, the bridge of consciousness was apparently broken or obstructed by shock, anaesthetics, or disease, the physical body becoming an empty tenement, with a vague caretaker keeping it just alive.

In one instance a man of materialistic views discovered himself standing in the far corner of the room, looking at his body in the chair. He saw the anaesthetist and dentist at work and, curiously enough, understood what they were saying to each other. He counted his teeth as they were pulled out, though he felt no pain from the operation. He knew that he was alive and thinking though separated in space from his body. When he returned to consciousness in his body, he mystified the two men by telling them what they had said to each other while he was deep under the gas.

In another case, a medical man took passage in an aircraft which crashed on landing. He saw the accident about to happen, felt the jolt, and found himself scrambling out of the wreckage. He saw that the pilot was pinned under the engine, and as mechanics rushed up and tried to release him, he tried two or three times to make them listen to his advice to lift the engine off the pilot first. He failed to make any impression, and it was as if they did not know he was there. Then he saw another man bending over a prostrate body and pouring something into its mouth. When he went up to investigate he recognized the body as his own. Then suddenly he 'came to' in the body, with his mouth full of sal volatile or brandy. His comment was, 'I don't mind dying, because I have already died once, and I know what it is like.'

Further descriptions which go into much detail and which have about them the quality of very real experiences will be found in *The Glimpse* by Arnold Bennett, *Corporal Tune* by L. A. G. Strong, and a number of other stories. Many subtle touches in these books suggest that the writers were deeply influenced by their psychic temperament and undoubtedly had some knowledge of these things. Such experiences, taken in bulk, provide circumstantial evidence that man's psyche is an organic functioning entity which links up closely with his physical body, but which can exist and act independently of it. This, of course, is a matter of constant research by scientists. Let us add that we are not concerned here with the question of survival after death, though this question may be germane to the matter, but simply with the functioning of the psyche, or soul, as an organism, even apart from the dense physical frame.

In studying the psyche in this light there are two points to be considered:

(a) The nature of the bridge which links the physical body with the psychic mechanism, and which therefore links the physical, or waking, with the psychic consciousness.

(b) The structure of the psychic mechanism itself.

The psycho-physical bridge mechanism belongs to the order of phenomena which take place in the electro-magnetic field associated with biochemical changes. All living organisms are known to produce such electro-magnetic phenomena—they are spoken of in such terms as 'nervous discharge'—and these take place within the orbit of the bridge mechanism. At one time, certain scientists, notably Sir Oliver Lodge, claimed that, besides solids, liquids, and gases, there existed a fourth state of matter which they called the ether. Science has since shifted its ground, and the simple conception of the ether has followed the simple though useful conception of the atom into semi-oblivon. For the ether there has been substituted a general conception of fields of force within which certain dynamic patterns, such as matter and radiation are observed. This, however, may be only a temporary dethronement, as Dirac and some other scientists once more feel the need for an ether to explain certain phenomena of matter.

The bridge mechanism, like other electro-magnetic

phenomena, exists in this field. It is probable that the dual quality of the field, as energy-matter, is the very thing which enables it to act as the bridge between the world of dense matter and the world of consciousness, and to bring the two together so that one can react on the other. Some writers have, in accordance with older scientific ideas, termed the bridge 'etheric', and we retain this term because of its convenience, and in spite of the change in outlook as to the nature of this 'ether'.

Evidence is accumulating for the existence of this etheric bridge. Many psychic observers speak about an aura or emanation which they say stands out from and around the body. Descriptions vary; some describe it as an ovoid or ellipsoid, while Æ, the Irish poet and visionary, describes only something like the feathered head-dress of the Red Indian. The only evidence approaching the scientific is that produced by the late Dr. Kilner of St. Thomas's Hospital with the help of dicyanin screens. His published work is incomplete, and Kilner died before he had gone further into it. In his book[1] he describes a subtle fringe extending a few inches beyond the physical frame and varying in health and disease, both in its quality and its shape.

This work of Kilner's, embryonic as it was, suggests that the aura he saw was not merely a cloud of matter, but was organized and reactive. The investigations of others all point to the aura as being more in the nature of an electric or magnetic field rather than anything denser, such as gases or fine chemical material. It seems to be a

---

[1] *The Human Atmosphere.* Other investigations are, for the most part, in the form of unpublished papers on diagnosis by means of pendulums, divining rods, and various forms of electrical or quasi-electrical apparatus. It is difficult to give references, or to find material of a sufficiently high scientific calibre to quote from.

field of energy with lines of force and does not consist of solid, liquid, or gaseous matter. This is as far as scientific investigation has yet taken us.

Clairvoyant observation confirms Kilner's descriptions but describes in the etheric double many details which Kilner had not reached. Not only does the double surround the physical body but it apparently penetrates throughout its structure. In fact, the double is described as itself a body somewhat larger than the dense physical so that the latter is like a kernel of heavier matter within the etheric matrix. The appearance it gives of being an aura or surround of the physical body is thus somewhat misleading.

Closer investigation suggests that the double consists of energy-matter of various densities. The denser layers are almost visible to the eye, and a very slight extension of normal vision is needed to see it. For instance, if, in a dim light, we touch the tips of the fingers together and then separate the hands it is frequently possible to see streamers of faint greyish mist emanating from the finger-tips. These emanations separate from one another and remain as radiating extensions of the fingers, and if we then spread the fingers of one hand apart each streamer is seen to remain in line with the length of the finger, spreading outwards like the ribs of a fan. This tends to prove that we are not dealing merely with light reflected from the finger-tips or with a retinal image, but with something different.

It needs a certain knack to observe this phenomenon, and the emanations are more easily seen if the hands are held against a dark background. The eye has to be, as it were, thrown a little out of focus; or else one looks at the hands 'out of the corner of the eye', for reasons already explained. A more elaborate technique, on which some experimental work was done, was to place the hands in a beam of ultra-violet rays passed through special filters, so that the amount of ordinary light was almost nil. By this means many people have been enabled to see, more clearly and easily than usual, some of the phenomena described above.[1]

If this etheric vehicle is a body with its own organs, metabolism, and nutritional functions, it exists more in terms of moving streams of energy than by virtue of any fixed structure. If we can picture the electric currents and magnetic fields in a wireless set as continuing to flow and to maintain their ordinary relationships after separation from the wires, valves, and other parts of the physical apparatus itself, we get a good illustration of what this means. The difference is that, so far as the etheric body is concerned, the energy-structure seems to exist first, and the dense physical body is, so to speak, condensed around and within the etheric and remains dependent upon it for its continued existence. In the case of an electrical machine the physical structure goes on existing even when it is 'dead', as we say, because the current is switched off. But the living organism does not go on as such when the etheric currents stop functioning. It rapidly decays; that is, it stops working as a single unit and, instead, each cell, and ultimately every chemical molecule, starts to live its own individual life instead of behaving as a member of an organized community, the body. It is the presence or absence of the etheric matrix which makes for bodily life, and death occurs when it is withdrawn, so justifying the name of vital body sometimes applied to the etheric form.

The dense body has a circulation of blood which contains in it matter in various states: there are solid corpuscles, there is liquid plasma, and there are gases loosely

[1] Ref. *Man Incarnate*—A Study in Vitality and Consciousness, by the present writers—(Theosophical Publishing House, London).

adherent to the haemoglobin in the corpuscles. The etheric organism apparently has a comparable circulation in which, also, different 'states' of energy-matter can be distinguished. The descriptions which follow are taken from the accumulated records of clairvoyant observation, and sum up the material common to the majority of such descriptions as are sufficiently clear and apparently objective. It should be added, moreover, that these too largely agree with what is to be found in traditional writings on the same subject. For present purposes, we need only divide these energies into two categories: the one, so to speak, nutritive, the other concerned with sensori-motor activities. The nutritive energy does not enter into our study, but details can be gleaned about it from Hindu books on Prana. The sensori-motor energy is of a different order, and shows itself in connection with two main functions: the first being physical sensation and action, the second, psychic activity. The psychic functions have an organization of their own which, being germane to this study, we shall describe in greater detail. The function of etheric circulation concerned with physical sensation and action is the nervous energy of the physiologist. It is not merely a vague flux, but is organized and directed; it has a rhythm or pulse connected with the breath—hence the importance of breathing in maintaining health and physiological balance—and it flows in specific channels. These channels correspond to the physical nerves, the nutritive energy flowing especially in the myelin sheath around the nerve fibres, while the sensori-motor energy flows through the fibre itself.

Under an anaesthetic, or in unconsciousness due to physical illness or shock, and in conditions of deep hypnotic trance, the normal relationship of the etheric to the dense organism is suspended, the subtler part of the etheric structure being dislocated or displaced until consciousness returns. During this period the physical body is kept alive by a link between the two, along which a greatly reduced measure of vital force still flows, like the thin stream of water along a choked pipe, or a flow of electricity through a loose but unbroken connection. If the connection is entirely lost, death occurs: the 'Silver Cord' of the Preacher is loosed.

During the earlier phases of spiritualism and psychical research there seems to have been a considerable amount of what is known as materialization. Forms, both inchoate and recognizable as human figures were photographed, touched and even weighed, and a great deal of early research is given over to accounts and discussion of these and other physical phenomena. To-day, however, *genuine* phenomena of this order are much less in evidence, and when one hears of them they rarely bear investigation. But when they do occur, they take a heavy toll of the etheric body of the medium and to some extent of the sitters. Ectoplasm, the psychic material so often seen and felt at séances, is actually etheric material drawn from the bodies of the medium and those around him by unseen operators who know how to mould and fashion it to suit their purposes. This material belongs to the medium's body, and so long as he is alive it is still attached to him by habit and use, and possibly by tenuous connections. When released by the materializing entity it is automatically drawn back to its source. The result of such withdrawal is often deep fatigue and other undesirable symptoms. More about this particular subject can be learned from the many books on materializing mediumship.[1]

The factors constituting physical perception have been clearly analysed. An external stimulus strikes a particular

[1] See *This World and That*, by the present writers.

sense organ and sends an impulse along the sensory nerve fibres to the spinal cord and thence to the brain. Here, according to physiologists, it becomes cognized as heat, light, sound, etc. In the process, memories of similar or contrasting experiences, and feelings of pleasure or aversion, weave in with the impression aroused, and may be joined by other sense stimuli. The total of this registers in consciousness and becomes a percept. If it does *not* register in consciousness, it is not a percept, but may still cause a reaction. For instance, if one is deep in absorbing talk one may push one's chair back from a fire which is uncomfortably hot without being conscious of what one is doing. The same process has taken place as for conscious perception, except that the reaction has been automatic instead of being deliberately reasoned out.

If, however, mind and brain are not the same, the processes in the latter are followed by transmission from the physical level to the mental organism where, as in our diagram (see p. 54) the *ego*, the perceiver, resides. Only then does it become a percept. There is, moreover, evidence that unconscious perception of physical objects takes place, and that this can be made conscious by special techniques.

This point is important because it shows that physical consciousness is a field where only certain mental acts become known, a window into the mind, through which a limited part of that mind becomes, as we say, conscious.

When we come to psychic perception, it is the mind itself which, as the Indian yogi and psychologist, Patanjali, puts it, acts as a sense. External psychic stimuli impinge on it, and the knower—the *ego*—perceives these, in so far as the mind is sensitive and reactive to them. It is therefore on a par with the physical senses, which can be dull or acute according to circumstances.

There are, however, two points of difference from physical perception: one, that nothing has passed from the plane of waking or physical consciousness into the mind. Hence, to become aware of psychic percepts 'from cold' is made more difficult. There is no facilitating path from the physical organism to make the perceiving easy. The other is that mental perception is pure cognition, and can be expressed only as 'I know'. It is only when bringing the knowledge into waking consciousness that it becomes translated into the language of one of the senses such as vision, hearing or touch, producing clairvoyance, clair-audience, etc.

Like primitive physical sensation, primitive psychic perception, in common with other mental processes is an undifferentiated function. It is for one thing inextricably mixed up with physical sensation, while the actual modes of perception are equally indistinct. If one tries to get a primitive person to tell one *how* he knows a certain thing, he will find it very difficult to analyse it out. The presence of a wild animal for instance may be detected by sight, smell and hearing, and the developed mind will find it fairly easy to say how much of each sense came into his awareness of it. The savage, on the other hand, will find this much more difficult: it is enough for him that he knows and he will not be able to give you details as to how that knowledge was reached.

So it is with psychism: the earlier forms are inchoate and confused, even if the net result of both physical and psychic perception aggregates into clear knowledge of a situation. Differentiation seems to take place only as a secondary stage, when it becomes translated into the language of the physical senses, following the line of least resistance. That is to say, a person naturally of the visual type will tend to be clairvoyant, one whose natural bent is towards sound or music, clairaudient, and so on. One highly trained clairvoyante, for instance, had physical vision so highly developed that if she wanted to match a piece of material for a dress, she did not need to take a sample with her but could go to a shop without the dress and pick out the right shade without trouble. As against this, another person who had no particular bias towards one sense or the other and in fact was decidedly diffuse in that he appreciated things through several channels and not particularly well through any of them, found that as his psychism changed from negative to positive, he became aware of psychic conditions in a direct way. After this it did not much matter to him whether he said that 'So-and-so's aura curled', in visual terms, or that 'He smelt psychically vile', or 'He was psychically so noisy'.

One of the things which is generally recognized by clairvoyants is that in the aura there are certain centres which appear to act, *not* as organs of psychic perception (the mind itself does that) but as channels by which these perception—and, for that matter, all psychic activity apart from perception—becomes related to the physical nervous system, and hence, in some cases, to conscious life.

The description which follows is a study of certain channels of psychic perception as seen by clairvoyance. It is backed by ancient tradition at least in general terms. It is not in line with the conclusions so far reached by laboratory workers in parapsychology. J. B. Rhine, for instance, states that he finds no evidence of localization of the faculty of extra-sensory perception, but that it appears in consciousness without any suggestion that it has come through any particular channel. The reason for this may be that laboratory subjects are positive and alert, and that this deletes the localized subjective sensations which are very characteristic where negative psychism is allied with positive and differentiated physical sensation. For the usual medium or psychometrist will hold an object to the head, or he may feel things in the region of the pit of the stomach, thus suggesting a focus for his perceptive function. But the positive psychic does not need to place the object he is studying anywhere; and in so far as he may localize the function, he places it in the middle of the head, perhaps in the region of the hypothalamus.

Each of these psychic organs, looked at clairvoyantly, is described as roughly in the shape of a cornucopia, with its narrow end based at a critical point in the physical spinal cord, and its mouth extending to the edge of the etheric aura. This mouth has a protective covering, a very fine membrane of psychic matter which is stretched across the opening, as one might stretch a piece of muslin across the horn of a loudspeaker to keep the dust out. The membrane is itself without function in perception, and fulfils the same essentially protective role as the conjunctival membrane covering the cornea of the eye, which is transparent and plays no part in seeing: yet the good health of the eye depends upon the conjunctiva and the cornea being intact.

Closer observation suggests that the cornucopial shape is due not to a fixed structure but to the play of two streams of psychic energy weaving together. One of these, flowing in the spinal cord, is thrown out from the centre and flows towards the periphery in a widening spiral; this represents the motor stream. The second stream, impinging on the surface of the etheric body, spirals inward, narrowing as it goes; this is the receptive or sensory stream. These two spirals flow parallel to one another, but in opposite directions, and may be compared to interlocking screw-threads, in that one may be said to run in the grooves of the other. They give an impression of spinning, like the fluid in the vortex of a whirlpool. It is this characteristic rotary movement which gives these centres their Sanskrit name of 'chakras' or wheels. The above is, of course, a very simple description of a highly complex structure; but it must serve.

When a physical nerve and sense-organ are called into activity, physiological research has shown that electrical changes occur in them. In the same way a psychic sense-organ becomes more highly charged when it becomes active. Its voltage, so to speak, rises; attention and intention leading, as one might expect, to a concentration of energy in the particular organ affected. The chakras thus appear as highly sensitive, vital parts of the mechanism, responsive to every change in the life and activity of the individual. At every mental or emotional movement, one or other chakra in the body lights up and expands, while another becomes more quiescent, and within each chakra changes occur as the balance of energies within it oscillates between a relatively greater state of outgoing or of receptive activity.

In primitive psychism the chakras appear to work in much the same way as the physical sense organs. That is to say that the individual consciousness is to be found at the central, narrow end of the funnel, and the objective psychic world is at the other end. The funnel itself makes the link between the two. It is like the physical eye: here, the objective physical world lies outside and beyond the covering membrane of the conjunctiva. Light passes through this, becomes focused within the structure of the eye itself, and reaches the retina. Thence it passes by means of the optic nerve, no longer as light but as nerve-impulses, to reach the individual consciousness.

MECHANISM

When psychism passes to a positive state the process seems to be reversed. It is as if the mind itself perceived directly and the percept then went, so to speak from within outward into physical consciousness. The chakra thus functions less as a perceptive organ than as the bridge between mind perceptively active in its own right and the consciousness of the physical brain.

There is thus a marked difference between the two kinds of psychism, the one negative, primitive and protopathic, the other positive and epicritic. The one belongs to the evolutionary phase preceding the establishment of the conscious ego, the latter to that which comes after this. Further, negative psychism seems to work in the human being as in the insects and lower animals, at the level of the sympathetic nervous system, with the 'solar' or more accurately coeliac plexus as its 'brain', the latter through the cerebro-spinal system with its focus in the cerebrum.

The linking up of psychic perception with the sympathetic system at its earlier levels is both traditional and observed by psychics to-day. But there is a point regarding this which is still obscure. For while bees and ants seem to be highly responsive to extra-sensory impulses, they can scarcely be said to be *conscious* of them. In the human being moreover, there are no direct sensory nerve-paths from the sympathetic system to the cerebro-spinal through which alone we become aware of things. There are, it is true, afferent nerves in the sympathetic, carrying impulses from the periphery towards the centre. But they do not carry anything which leads to sense perception. So that there seems to be a link missing in our knowledge of the chain of reaction which nevertheless allows negative psychic impulses impinging on the sympathetic system to reach consciousness.

It is at once logic and an observed fact that one sees

reflected in the chakra structure what we have already discussed in general psychological terms in Chapter II: the process of separation between the subjective and objective worlds which occurs as the intellect develops. But the space thus made by the mind between subject and object would, by reason of its polarization, contain a magnetic field, and it is in such conditions that growth and the birth of new mental capacities take place.

It should, however, be remembered that a person can be intellectually objective in one part of his life, but unfocused, confused, and entangled in another. It is only when he applies his power of thought, judgment, and observation to any part of the field that he learns to separate himself from the objects in that field and become clear and objective to it. The same must apply to the psychic field: as a person begins to pay attention to it, he introduces a positive factor into the automatic and unfocused activity of his psychic mechanism, which not only makes him aware of that activity, but also makes that mechanism a better and finer piece of apparatus for his use.

This would explain how it is that the deliberate use and study of one's psychic nature in a scientific and critical way would actually enhance and develop that side of oneself. And, in so far as it had been left behind the rest of one's psychological development, it would help to locate and cure the troubles which it causes by being still in its primitive and uncoordinated state.

The chakras are the main avenues by which mental or emotional impulses pass between the physical waking consciousness and the psychic realm, whether these originate in the external psychic or the internal psychological spheres. To illustrate this point: a person may either state that he is totally unaware of any superphysical experience, or he may—as occurs in certain psychological states—

complain that he is incapable of feeling his own emotions. In both cases the condition is one in which the chakras in the bridge-mechanism are not responsive or are not functioning freely.

There are, as has been implied above, a number of chakras. Those most used in psychic perceptivity to-day are: one, at the pit of the stomach, related to the solar, or coeliac, plexus and its immediate spinal connections; one whose mouth is in the region of the heart; one at the throat, with its root probably in the *medulla oblongata*; one, between the eyebrows, related to the pituitary gland and the third ventricle of the brain; and one at the vertex of the head, connected with the pineal body and also with the third ventricle. The last two are found symbolically represented in effigies of those who are supposed to be spiritually enlightened, by the uraeus in Egyptian art, and the Hindu caste marks; while the royal crown, the saint's halo, and the curious pyramid so often found in Buddhist sculptures, refer to the pineal centre. Tradition also tells of two more chakras, one at the base of the spine, connected with the *kundalini* or the serpent-fire, and one over the spleen, connected with physical vitality. These two are known to clairvoyants. As, however, their perceptive functions—if any—are not known, they do not concern us in this study.

The different chakras are, as one would expect, described as being used for registering different types of psychic sensations. We use the eye to sense form, colour, movement; the ear for sound, and so on. Similarly, special psychic centres correspond to particular kinds of sensation. The distinction should be kept clear between the type of sensation and the organ itself. The eye is the organ which senses light-impulses, but it is not the sense of sight. The ear carries sound-impulses, but it is not hearing. We can have experiences of sight and sound quite apart from these organs, for we can imagine a scene or a landscape and 'see' it full of light, colour, and movement, or we can 'hear' a conversation or music which takes place solely in our own minds: eye and ear are not affected, and, in fact, such imaginative activities often take place best in the dark or in a quiet place. Similarity, where psychic perception is concerned, it is often found that this is easiest when the physical organs are at rest: a clairvoyant often prefers to work with his eyes closed, so as not to find his psychic sight confused by the impacts from physical sight.

In the physical world it is fairly easy to distinguish between what we see, hear, smell, feel, or taste. Yet, originally biologists tell us, physical sensation was a diffuse, undifferentiated sense of touch belonging to the whole skin. Only gradually and by a long process of evolution were special senses—sight, hearing, and the rest—developed. The skin adapted itself in special areas to form the eye, the ear, and other specialized organs. Eventually, no doubt, psychic perception will become as clear-cut and differentiated as physical now is.

Roughly speaking, the correspondence between the psychic counterpart of the physical senses and particular centres is as follows: the solar, or coeliac, plexus is that of feeling; the throat, that of psychic hearing; the head chakras, those of vision. Taste appears as yet to have no psychic counterpart, and the sense of smell is a peculiar one in that very few people are able to distinguish between psychic and subtle physical smells. Yet despite the fact that at the sensory end of the range psychic perceptivity takes on a quasi-sensory quality, it should always be borne in mind that the pure, mental psychic sense is simple, direct cognition of the kind many sensitive writers, artists, and others have.

These descriptions are both empirical and traditional.

MECHANISM

They have indirect confirmation in that an overworked clairvoyant gets bad headaches, a clairaudient is prone to throat trouble, and the clair-sentient majority suffer from gastro-intestinal troubles and from general sympathetic difficulties. The heart chakra has a special function connected with intuition, understanding, insight, and comprehension—in short, with something beyond ordinary perception; it belongs to subjects to be dealt with in a later chapter. Despite all this, however, it should always be remembered that the mind perceives in terms of pure cognition or direct knowledge. The sensory elaboration is secondary to this.

The psyche, as we have said, can act, think, and feel independently from the body. But when these activities have to be brought through into the physical consciousness, the etheric bridge-mechanism leading from the psychic world to the physical is all-important. One end of the bridge is in the psychic world, and the other is in the central nervous system. There are two main thoroughfares across the bridge: one leads to that part of the nervous system called the sympathetic, and the other to the cerebro-spinal system. To be able to grasp the distinction between what has been called negative and positive psychism, it is important that we should have a clear picture of both these channels, and of the influence on the person concerned of what passes through each of them.

Conveniently for our study, Nature has developed the central nervous system of different orders of animals on two main lines. In the insects, the sympathetic system is paramount: there is no brain or spinal cord, and the creature is ruled by what, in the vertebrates, are the sympathetic ganglia. Vertebrates possess the sympathetic mechanism, but their higher activities are governed by the brain and spinal cord.

MECHANISM

When we speak of the 'solar plexus' it is necessary to make a distinction between two things. One is the solar plexus chakra, or psychic sense-organ for the diffuse sense-of touch or 'feeling'. The other is the plexus of nerves and ganglia which, virtually, make it the brain of the sympathetic nervous system.

In the second capacity, it is the accepted view that its function is that of co-ordinating the internal economy of the body. In this it works reciprocally with the para-sympathetic, or vagal, nervous system, the two together being called the autonomic system. The shifting balance between these two govern such things as blood pressure, digestion, the heartbeat, and, in general, the metabolism of the whole and of every individual part of the animal.

The cerebro-spinal system carries out the external activities of the vertebrate: sensation, movement, posture, balance, and all the many factors which govern its relationship to the outer world.

The respective roles of the autonomic and the cerebro-spinal systems remind one of those of the engineers and the deck officers of a ship. The engineering staff keep the ship running, obey orders to start and stop, to go slow or fast, and so on. Without them the ship would never leave or reach port. They do this without needing to know the course or position of the ship, or anything of what is happening outside or around it; the deck officers are completely in their hands as to the internal economy of the ship. The function of the deck officers is to deal with the things outside the ship, to see the land and other objects, and find their way about. They represent the cerebro-spinal system, whereas the engineers represent the sympathetic system, which works blindly and without being aware of things outside its own sphere.

These descriptions refer to the life of the animal in his

physical environment. They seem to apply equally to the relation between the animal and the psychic environment, though with some modification.

From the psychic angle, the solar plexus and its associated ganglia appear, in animals and undeveloped human psychics, to act as the centre for reception and co-ordination of primitive psychic sense-stimuli. These stimuli are essentially and primarily concerned with the instinctive life of the animal, and urge it to behave in such a way as to satisfy the instinct aroused. This necessitates the use, in the vertebrates, of much more of the nervous system than merely the autonomic. For an animal in the mating season or in the activities concerned with storing food against a hard winter, is using all the elaborate mechanism of movement and balance, vision, hearing, and smell, to satisfy his instinctive urges. In short, he is using his cerebro-spinal system in response to stimuli which appear to reach him via the solar plexus chakra, in the first place, and to spread from there along the connections of the solar ganglia throughout the nervous system.

That the results of psychic investigations in this matter seem correct appears to be borne out by the behaviour of insects. They, of all creatures, live on rigid instinctive patterns of behaviour from which they cannot depart, and which they have to follow blindly until the cycle of the pattern is fulfilled, or they die in the process. There can be no originality of behaviour among them. Moreover—and this is especially marked in the case of the hymenoptera which live in communities, such as bees, ants, and termites—they are highly sensitive to extra-sensory or psychic, impacts, which influence them very strongly and guide their behaviour along these instinctive lines. As already pointed out, they have no nervous system other than the sympathetic in which to receive these psychic impacts.

MECHANISM

The vertebrate, on the other hand, as he evolves, tends to develop individual freedom. He is at first largely tied down to rigid instinctive patterns, but the higher animals become increasingly able to depart from these patterns, and learn to adapt themselves to new conditions. The imperative commands of instinct become subdued, as individual desire, and, later, will, assert themselves. This applies slightly to the higher vertebrates, such as the dog, the elephant, and the ape, but more particularly to civilized man.

The vertebrate autonomic system is believed to contain no sensory fibres but to be a self-regulating motor system. The fact that these impulses arise depends on stimuli travelling to the cerebro-spinal system along ordinary sensory nerves, not through the sympathetic system itself. This seems to contradict the idea that extra-sensory impulses reaching the sympathetic 'brain' in the coeliac or solar plexus can reach consciousness in the cerebral cortex. The exact mechanism hence cannot be explained in neurological terms. But the fact remains that many 'negative' psychics do become aware of at least some of their extra-sensory percepts, though only in a rather inchoate manner.

It may be that the explanation lies in the fact that a very large part of the activity of the cerebro-spinal system, even in developed man, is automatic and subconscious. In this it seems to be an extension upward of the autonomic, though part of its activity—as for instance the contraction of antagonistic muscles which would normally balance one another by an automatic process—can be controlled by an effort of will. The autonomic proper cannot be so controlled. Conscious awareness is a late development in evolution and probably does not exist below the human level except in the highest animals. In neurological terms,

it is believed not to exist below the level of the optic thalamus in the brain; and there, as far as is known, it is primitive and partakes of the all-or-none quality of instinctive
reactions. It becomes *conscious*, so that the individual is
aware of it, but it still needs a further step before it becomes *self*-conscious, at the higher cortical level of the
brain. It is only when this level begins to function that
the individual has attained the beginning of the power to
know self from not-self and, consequently, to have a real
measure of freedom and self-direction.

If this is so, we shall readily understand why purely
primitive psychism is unconscious and manifests itself in
automatic reactions and behaviour. Only when the psychic
sense-impulses passing through the solar plexus ganglia
radiate far enough into the cerebro-spinal system to reach
the lowest conscious levels—i.e. the thalamic—does the
individual become aware of them. And even then it is only
in a primitive form, not under his control. If he then learns
to raise this consciousness to the cortical level, he becomes
analytical, and his perceptions become gradually more
objective. In doing this, he shifts his focus of psychic
attention, and a new mechanism comes into play. With
this, he gradually learns to receive psychic impacts directly
into the head and co-ordinate them there—traditionally,
at a focusing point in the third ventricle of the physical
brain—instead of in the solar plexus region. This also
leads to the motor activities resulting from his perceptions
being increasingly controlled and discriminating, like the
movement of the hand reaching out to an object one has
seen physically. At earlier stages, such movements are
largely automatic, and more in the nature of a reflex action
in response to psychic stimulation of the solar plexus.

MECHANISM

Human behaviour can be separated into two kinds: that which is automatic and instinctive, and that which is voluntary, self-controlled, and guided by conscious thought. The less developed the individual, the more automatic and insect-like is his behaviour. Savages and primitive types tend not only to be ruled by their instinctive urges but to fall into fixed patterns which repeat themselves every time a similar situation arises. Not only does the savage naturally tend to go to war when his aggressiveness is aroused, but he must prepare himself for it by going through elaborate and set ritual-forms and dances beforehand, because on their performance his success depends. The same applies to marriage and other activities in primitive communities. Among civilized men to-day there are still marked traces of these fixed patterns: custom decrees a preparation for and a ceremony of marriage even where the law does not, and the social ostracism of those who omit such preparations is too strong for most people. Yet there are many who feel intellectually that forms and observances are irrational and cannot of themselves make or prevent such a relationship as marriage. The same applies to many other social habits and customs, to which people automatically conform, but which have often no rational basis and which seem to the logical mind quite unnecessary.

At the other end of the scale from insect-behaviour is behaviour perfectly adapted to every changing set of circumstances, carried out in the clear light of awareness, and unmarred by irrelevant unconscious urges and desires.

When primitive man is self-aware, he realizes where his consciousness is focused. As one such man firmly asserted to a well-known psychologist, 'Anybody who says he does not think in his belly is a fool': he knew that the chief centre of his mental and emotional life was in the autonomic 'brain', the coeliac plexus, at the pit of the stomach. In contrast to this, we class the independent, original, far-seeing man whom we consider a superior product of our culture as 'a man of brains'.

In practice, civilized man to-day is still partly under the sway of primitive instinctive urges, and only partly governed by his conscious mind. He oscillates between the two.

Where psychic matters are concerned, then, a division similar to that of his psychological behaviour may be made. Negative psychism is uncontrolled, undifferentiated, primitive. It tends to 'all-or-none' reactions. It is usually not possible for the negative psychic to distinguish between the products of his own mind and actual psychic objects external to it. Its impacts rarely reach consciousness, and more often set up a chain of reaction which is quite unconscious. Its mechanism is linked to the autonomic nervous system, and in particular to the coeliac plexus. Positive psychism is consciously directed and controlled by the individual. It develops increasingly fine shades of discrimination and judgment, and the reaction to these is deliberate and chosen behaviour. Its mechanism is connected with the cerebro-spinal system, and is centred in the head, the coeliac plexus becoming secondary to this. The beginning of transition from the first to the second takes place when the intellect is applied to analysing and making conscious the impact on us of the psychic world.

The change from the first to the second stage is a gradual one. It is probable that the most primitive form of psychism is entirely unconscious: the individual reacts to impulses from the psychic world in a purely automatic way and without any conscious awareness of what he is doing. There is no evidence that insects have any consciousness of themselves, and their behaviour suggests that their lives are run on blind, automatic, instinctive lines. In the same way, the autonomic nervous system of vertebrates is, as the name itself indicates, one of automatic and unconscious reactions. We need to pay deliberate attention and make a definite effort to become aware of its workings, and then only some of its phenomena come into view: we may, if we pay attention, feel ourselves blush or pale, go hot or cold, notice our breath-rhythm alter, and so on; but we are never directly conscious of the contraction of the pupil of the eye, or of normal digestion. In the same way, purely negative reaction to psychic impulses remains unconscious throughout and is not perceived by the one who experiences it.

In the intermediate stage, the channel by which the impulse reaches the individual is still that part of the bridge-mechanism which is connected with the autonomic plexus. But here some measure of conscious awareness goes with it: the impulses reach the individual by an intermediate nervous mechanism between the autonomic system and the cerebral cortex—probably, though not certainly, connected with the optic thalamus and its tracts. The degree of consciousness varies a great deal with the individual, but, at best, the quality of psychic perception is uncertain and confused. Moreover, the percipient is not at this stage able to disentangle what he sees or feels in the objective psychic world from the contents of his own mind. That is to say, he may see an object in the psychic world which is quite independent of himself, but—just as occurs when he sees a physical object—his mind reacts to it, liking or disliking it, and evoking associations and memories of his own. These become linked with the object in the usual way of psychological associations, until they seem to become part of the object itself, and the percipient cannot tell what he has seen, and what he has added out of his own mind to the thing seen. This is the state of things where most mediums, and especially trance mediums, are concerned. Experience seems to confirm the claim that they really perceive things in the psychic world, but that, from the point of view of the investigator, they often spoil the clarity of their experience by clothing it in material of a personal nature and with feelings and ideas of their own.

At the other end of the scale, positive psychism is a purely objective sense. The percipient receives his knowledge through the brain, and it is as clear-cut and finely focused as physical perception through the cerebral cortex. There can be no confusion between what is perceived and the reaction of the percipient's mind to it, and the image is no more distorted than a fine microscope distorts the material placed beneath its lens.

It must be added at once that this is a point which few or none have reached. There is, even among the wisest of men, still a considerable personal element in all their perceptions and judgments, and this is all the more marked where psychic perception is concerned. In short, the majority of people are somewhere on the road between negative and positive psychism, just as they are on the road between instinctive herd-behaviour and the ideal of strong and free individual life. This would not matter if the whole of the individual were educated and developed to the same stage. But, as has been pointed out, psychological education is as yet far ahead of psychic education. Psychological education has, in short, made us increasingly 'men of brains', while the lack of psychic education has left us still in the state of being psychically speaking 'men of belly', or, more politely, of solar-coeliac plexus.

If the effort is made to learn by experience how to make psychic perceptions increasingly conscious, and to analyse them intellectually, the centre of sensitiveness gradually shifts from the coeliac plexus to the head centres. The receptive, automatic pattern is then changed to that of the self-controlled psychism, which, by virtue of our mental development, really belongs to our race. To coin terms to fit these two stages, sensibility becomes sensitivity. In the first stage, something akin to a reflex action takes place through the nervous system, but to a psychic, not a physical, stimulus. In the second stage, the solar plexus chakra is simply an organ for the psychic sense which corresponds to physical touch. It is a point of sensation, not a centre for instinctive reaction. The deliberate use of the intellect to analyse and study psychic perception is the factor which brings about this change of focus.

To illustrate roughly the difference between negative and positive psychic reactions, let us imagine a newly dead person who is bewildered and depressed at suddenly losing his physical body. He enters a room where the living occupants have different degrees of awareness, and each one responds in a way which depends on the level of his psychic development. The really negative person, whose psychic senses work in a primitive, undirected way, will most probably become depressed, perhaps feel cold and shivery, and may not be able to give an account of why he feels so. In any case, he will be quite unable to keep outside the depression which has invaded him. In contrast to this, a self-directed and self-contained psychic will observe the entrance of the 'dead' person as an external happening, and may say, unemotionally, 'A person out of the body has come into the room; he is confused and depressed, and does not like being without his physical body.' The psychic may also be able to give a tolerably clear description of the dead man, and possibly other details about him. The important point is that the latter will observe the facts as external to himself, and will not become entangled in the emotion emanating from the visitor, nor will he feel in any way identified with him.

This ability of the trained and positive psychic to analyse his observations is shown by the following story, given by a clairvoyant friend. She was asked to attend a lecture given by a well-known literary man, and asked if she would report upon any phenomena she happened to see during the lecture. She did not know the lecturer, nor had she any data to go upon. For some time the lecturer proceeded to discourse upon poetry in general and without any particular point being made; then the clairvoyant said that she noticed a luminous figure beginning to emerge from the left-hand side of the lecturer's aura. At first it was nothing but a column of vapoury matter like wreathing white mist. It ebbed and flowed, gradually assuming the first faint beginnings of a shape, and as the lecturer warmed to his subject the shape developed into a recognizable figure of a young man.

The lecturer led on towards his principal object, which was to extol the work of a particular modern poet for whom he felt a great admiration. As he did so, the vague figure at his side assumed a more definite shape, one vaguely familiar to the clairvoyant observer. Step by step it became more lifelike and acquired a certain animation.

'Now', said the lecturer, 'I will conclude by reading you a few of the poems written by X not long before he died,' and he went on to emphasize once again the beauty and depth of the mind which had written them. It was clear that his enthusiasm for the poet was not confined to his writings alone, but that he was also personally interested in him as a man.

As he went on, the psychic figure matured yet further. Suddenly, the clairvoyant recognized the likeness: it was an exact replica of a photograph of the young man which appeared at the beginning of his collected works. Later, when the lecture was over, and the speaker's mind turned to other matters—greeting friends, answering questions, and so on—the image gradually dissolved. It lost its definiteness and the material of which it was made streamed back into the aura of the lecturer, from which it had come.

It was not the soul of the poet himself, it was a lay figure generated by the thoughts and feelings of the lecturer. He had in his mind a picture of the poet, based on the photograph in the book, and, as he expressed his enthusiasm, he also, and quite literally, 'expressed' from himself the picture of the person he was speaking about.

Such a phenomenon is not uncommon, and at séances, when a medium tells someone in the audience that 'A tall woman with grey hair is standing beside you,' and gives details which make the person addressed say at once, 'That's my mother!' the odds are that this figure is a thought-image and not the 'dead' person at all.

The relevance of this story lies in that, to be able to discriminate clearly between such an image and a real 'dead' person requires a steadiness of the bridge-mechanism and of the mind behind it which the negative psychic does not possess. It is only when the bridge can be held steady and poised that the images perceived through it are well focused and undistorted, and details clearly noted. The etheric bridge actually functions like the screen of a magic lantern: it needs to be clean and smooth, not stained or creased. But the clarity of the image projected on it depends not only on this but on the other factors, most important of which is the ability of the intellect of the percipient to transmit and focus the image on the screen.

Incidentally, the main features which help to distinguish between a thought-image of a person and the person himself are mainly these:

(a) That there is almost always some imperfection or omission in a thought-form, and

(b) That, no matter how perfect the form, a certain quality is lacking in the thought-form, which the 'dead' person has. The difference may be very subtle, and on a par with that between a first-class waxwork and a live person. In this connection, one is reminded of the story of a visitor to a famous show, who, after asking his way from a wax figure, then proceeded to comment at length and very personally upon the looks of another immobile statue, which presently stood up and walked calmly away. Careful observation would have shown at least one matter which would have made such a mistake impossible—i.e. that the live person breathes. It may be that psychic accuracy depends on the ability to notice such a fine point as this: a matter obviously impossible unless the observer is capable of keeping the image clear and still.

(c) That a thought-form repeats its behaviour after a stereotyped pattern: sooner or later the same sequence recurs. A real person does not do this, whether he be 'alive' or 'dead', or, even if habits and mannerisms persist, he tends to introduce some variation in his ways. These show up quite clearly to careful observation.

A trained clairvoyant, observing the mechanism of a negative psychic, finds that in purely receptive psychism the structure of the etheric bridge is unstable, and the streams of energy in it are very easily influenced by external stimuli or by personal feelings which deflect them from their normal course, with the result that abnormal eddies and cross-currents occur. These eddies may apparently be the basic cause of a great deal of psychic ill health. Under such conditions, perception is naturally confused

MECHANISM

and bewildering, and the unfortunate subject is like a person standing on a refuge between opposite streams of traffic in a busy street. The uncontrollable reactions of the etheric bridge affect the chakras, and the individual is left at the mercy both of unconscious psychological reactions and of external psychic influences playing upon an over-sensitized mechanism. In the case of the positive psychic, the energy and movement of the chakras would be directed from within, by the self, or 'I'. In other words, the chakras of the negative are like a windmill, responsive to every breeze, whereas those of the positive are like an electrically-driven fan: capable of generating their own wind as well as being sensitive to draughts blowing upon them.

The first force generally used to control the reaction of a chakra to stimuli is the intellect positively directed. This steadies and holds the alignment of the out-going spiral of energy. In the purely receptive chakra of the negative psychic, the incoming and outgoing streams are not co-ordinated with one another. The result is a lack of tone, of resilience, in the mechanism. When the intellect comes into play, the two streams become polarized, and lines of force are then created which help to maintain a stable relationship between the two streams. The difference is roughly that between the canvas cone used on airfields as a wind indicator and a metal horn on a loudspeaker: the first goes slack when not filled with wind coming from outside, while the second retains its shape and does not depend on fortuitous external factors.

CHAPTER V

Mechanism—II

The Mind: Thinking and Feeling

The function of the etheric mechanism is to act as the bridge between man and the objective physical world. Over it travel impulses from this world to the mind, which result in perception of the physical world. In reverse direction, impulses from the mind lead to action.

But besides this, as we have already said, extra-sensory percepts are also conveyed over this bridge when they enter waking consciousness. These manifest in two ways. One, the commonest, is where the actual percept does not become conscious, but action results. Instinctive acts involving more than simple nervous reflexes seem to be based on a collective mandate from Nature to the species or variety, and cause action-patterns which are characteristic of the creature. True, the immediate cause of the action-chain may be physical—as when an animal sees danger, or spring urges it to build a typical nest; but the exact pattern of this chain seems less to be learned than acquired from behind the scenes in some way independent of learning or direct imitation. The view that instinct and extra-sensory perception are interlinked is suggested not only from a study of the latter, but also from the biological angle, and, indeed, was put forward recently by Professor Hardy, of Oxford, at the British Association.

Human beings also have instinctive urges, unlearned

and unsuggested by others. Some of these are primitive and simple, like the sucking-reflex of babies, but others are highly complex and are in fact the basis of civilized, communal living. Such group, collective, or herd impulses appear to be dependent on communication between mind and mind, usually unconscious and behind the scenes of maternal life. They result in action which may, in its details, be highly individual and determined by personal choice, or it may be of an automatic kind in which rational choice and volition has little or no part. Thus patriotism, the natural reaction of a citizen to a national situation, is often automatic and may override rational considerations or the justice of the cause one feels one must defend. This and many other collective movements work in like manner, showing a certain cohesion of minds which is regardless of heredity or education and seems to depend at least partly on physical proximity.

Jung, speaking of the collective mind, has said that if a person lives for a few years in a certain community, he willy-nilly to some extent becomes a member of that community, becomes 'naturalized' into it—and that, even if he still consciously associates himself with a previous national or a racial group. This is borne out by facts such as that the American city-dwelling negro, even in the Deep South, where he is shunned by the whites, develops mental patterns profoundly affected by western thought. This is found not to be due solely to a different way of life. The new patterns are in good measure different from those of denizens of the same race in the African bush. Research in psychiatry shows that, physical habits apart, the American negro is inwardly westernized despite living in squalor and despite pure African heredity.

So it seems that, whether we speak of the collective with Jung, or the herd instinct with Wilfred Trotter, we have to do with phenomena of direct, if unseen, and un-conscious, psychic communication between mind and mind.

It is therefore reasonable to postulate that the individual mind can both perceive and act *at its own level*, where it both influences and is influenced by other individual minds. It is not necessary to know in waking conscious-ness what is going on. Indeed, if one studies human be-haviour, it seems that unconscious extra-sensory percep-tion is probably the most potent and constant form of communication between individuals and groups: far more so than conscious interchange in waking consciousness, whether in words or acts. Telepathy, in other words, is quite the commonest form of speech—but, owing to its merciful silence, we do not know it.

The reason is in the fact already stated that waking con-sciousness represents only a minute fraction of the whole field of mental activity. It depends on the etheric bridge which brings the mind into direct contact with the dense physical world in so far as it is able to carry messages be-tween the two. The bridge itself is not conscious: con-sciousness is an attribute of the mind (psyche or soul) where the *ego* is centred, not of the bridge mechanism it-self, any more than the eye or the ear can be said to be conscious apart from that mind.

The focus of consciousness can be temporarily any-where within a wide range of levels of being. In waking consciousness, it is concentrated at the level of the dense physical world, while in sleep it largely retires 'within' the psyche, loosening its link with that world.

The etheric bridge is thus a conveyor of impulses. But it is also an inhibitor. It would seem indeed as if clear physical consciousness of physical objects is achieved only by a process of deletion. This not only cuts off overtones of psychic awareness of that object, it also hides the complex of processes which take place between the receipt of sense data and the formulation of thoughts about them in consciousness. Thus our eyes receive certain light stimuli and we say, 'That is a beautiful rose'. But we do not know what goes on behind the scenes to produce that simple acknowledgement, calling up memories, feelings, associations, and so on. It is as if the senses fed data into a computing machine, which then presents the operator with the answer without his having to follow the intricacies of calculation needed to reach it.

This indicates the nature of 'psychism'. It is the ability of the mind to act as a sense at its own level—which, in a more or less co-ordinated way it does all the time: the collective is always with us and influencing us, whether we know it or not. But in addition, the difference between the psychic and the non-psychic person is the degree of conductivity of the etheric bridge in bringing percepts from the mental level into the waking conscious field.

Thus the quality of psychic awareness will be determined by two factors: one the sensitivity of the mental equipment at its own level (a thing very marked in every cultured and artistic person), the other the adequacy of the channel between the mind and waking consciousness. These factors are often related, a clear, sensitive mind giving clear, conscious psychic awareness, while a muddled, disordered mind will reflect its own confusion in consciousness. At the same time, lack of sensitivity of the etheric mechanism itself blots out much of what the mind may perceive, so that only under abnormal conditions—drugs, dissociation, illness, etc.—does the veil thin and direct psychical awareness is possible.[1]

[1] Mr. Aldous Huxley, in *The Doors of Perception*, gives a very good example of this. His visions reflect the quality of Mr. Huxley's own mind,

MECHANISM

There is a certain tradition in occultism that man's dense physical body is not really a human principle. It belongs to the sub-human animal kingdom, and is borrowed from this kingdom and adapted to human ends. If this is true, it is highly suggestive. For it would give us a reason for thinking of physical matter as 'real'—i.e. a place of *rera* or objects—whereas the rest of the universe is not real. The physical world, considered from this angle, is outside the human field, the rest is within it, and this makes a vast difference to our ordinary perceptions.

It is evident, however, that the animal body depends on mind for its existence: indeed, the whole of the animal mind is orientated to this end, carrying out the mandates of instinct, making certain choices and judgments within the framework of these mandates. And man, together with the animal body, has had to take over the mind which belongs to it. But, being man, he brings something more to bear: the human element, which not only has a focus of I-ness, the *ego* which the animal lacks, but teleological urges derived from what we call the spiritual realm, taking him away from merely animal, utilitarian living, into philosophy, religion, a search for self-realization and true meaning.

That these two forces are often in conflict is obvious to any student of psychology, causing turmoil and distress. Compared to this stormy sea, physical consciousness is like a tranquil lake. It gives an anchorage on to something which does not shift as our minds shift, or if it shifts, does so relatively slowly. In this way, we have been able to establish in this level a place of clear focus and sharp

though it was only through the effects of the mescalin that he became conscious of things beyond the normal senses, in a manner recognizable to any good psychic. It also shows why others have not been so successful in their experiments with this highly dangerous drug.

images. Moreover, it has supplied us with a fulcrum against which we have been to some extent able to press in order to lift our sense of selfhood and identity clear of the mass consciousness of animal life.

Hence it is scarcely to be wondered that our conceptual language about non-physical things relies on the stable, clear-cut imagery of this physical world. And indeed, despite the cautions already uttered that the way we see things is certainly not to see them as they are, our description of the mind as seen by clairvoyance has to be couched in terms which, if not true in any absolute sense, have pragmatic value.

All the above is a preamble to a consideration of mind itself, from the viewpoint of the psychic investigator. For many clairvoyants speak of it as a *thing*, as a three-dimensional body which moves from place to place and within which changes of shape and pattern occur. It is influenced by the mental world which surrounds it, and, in turn, it reacts on this world and produces changes in it. These changes, moreover, are not instantaneous, but take time— even though that time is infinitesimal compared to the time taken by physical movements on the same scale. In short, it behaves as does a material body in the physical world, although it does not belong to that world. This suggests that, while the psychologist looks at the mind from the inside and sees it in terms of function, the psychic sees it from outside in such a way that it seems to be a material structure existing in space and time.

Mind is, moreover, often spoken of as a 'vesture' of the indwelling Self or the Thinker behind thought. Described in visual terms, it constitutes what is called the aura. The

aura is thus said to be the psychic, as distinct from the physical, body; and just as physical consciousness functions in and through the physical frame, so does psychic consciousness play in and through the aura, its business being to convey information regarding experience at the psychic level to the self, or 'I'. The word 'aura' is convenient because it is in general use.

That it is in reality, and apart from perception of it in physical consciousness, just as it appears is, of course, highly doubtful. Indeed, it is probably a field of subtle and complex electro-magnetic waves which, though organized and ordered, only acquires geometric form when it impinges on the material world—just as a beam of light only appears as a luminous disc when it reaches the screen on which it is thrown. The lighted disc is nevertheless related to the field of energy which produces it. The same principle would, of course, apply to 'thought-forms', too.

Can we go further in trying to see the mind in its own realm, and apart from its contact with the physical world? If the principles outlined in Chapter II are correct, it can be conceived as a field of force focused round a non-dimensional centre which we know as *ego* or Self, according to which aspect of it we are looking at. This field extends towards the physical world. In other words, it starts from one energy-level and progressively reflects into more 'earthy' energy-levels, more material form, where it becomes perceptible to the clairvoyant. In other words, both the psychologist who sees mind only in abstract, energetic terms, and the clairvoyant who speaks of form, are right: but only partly right.

For descriptive purposes, we shall, however, go on using the dimensional picture, with whatever mental reservations we keep in mind.

MECHANISM

It is most important that the principle should be clearly grasped that the self, or 'I', works in and through the aura and the dense physical body, but that it exists apart from both. The mental aura and the dense body are what is called the personality, a name derived from the *persona*, the mask once worn by the classical actor, and suggests consequently that behind that mask there is a real actor, or self. Unless this is understood, no real grasp of psychic— or, for that matter, psychological—problems can be reached. Moreover, the descriptions which follow would then appear to be purely materialistic and devoid of the sense of something beyond.

To sum up the points suggested above:

(a) There is a thinker, or self, behind thought and feeling.[1]

(b) This self uses a subtle, but from one aspect material, psychic organism, as well as a dense physical body.

(c) The psychic organism is the place of the psychic-psychological functions, as the physical is the vehicle for physical experience.

(d) The psychic organism is not contained spatially or functionally within the physical frame but extends beyond it.

(e) Since we are capable of psychic perception while in full waking consciousness, it is evident that a close link exists between the psychic and physical organisms. The link is the etheric bridge, or body.[2]

To the clairvoyant, the aura generally appears to be an

---

[1] Thouless and Wiesner have suggested the term 'Shin'—the name of a Hebrew letter—to denote this thinker.

[2] The psyche or mind should not be identified with Spirit. Spirit is mysterious and transcendental. Mind may have its mysterious aspect, but it is not transcendental.

ellipsoid or ovoid form of which the outer limit is some-where from two to three feet from the physical skin. The distance must be taken very roughly, as the size varies enormously, both accordingly to the individual observed and to the expansive or retiring state of his mind at the particular moment. It appears solid, in the sense that it is not merely a shell but a three-dimensional object with matter inside it. A general view before the details are sorted out gives the impression of it as a form full of moving streams and wreaths of coloured vapour, con-stantly flowing and changing, expanding and contracting. Probably there will be parts where the colours appear to be more static and tend to repeat themselves, while other parts are active and changing. Within the ovoid, occa-sional shapes and designs, sometimes neat and clear, some-times vague and fuzzy, appear and dissolve, or they may be pushed out of the aura and float away into space. Some auras are shining and coruscating, like a soap bubble in the sunlight, others are dull and leaden. As one watches, the character of an aura may quite suddenly change, a quiet one may spring into activity, while another, hitherto wide and harmonious, may suddenly shrink up like a sea-anemone and lose its bright colours. In short, what is seen is the picture of a highly sensitive, dynamic organism which responds instantly to every change of thought and feeling in the person concerned. Indeed, the trained clair-voyant sees the aura shifting its appearance, just as shifting expressions alter a person's face, but the variations take place on a larger scale because the aura is so much more plastic and responsive.

It can be said in broad terms that the *form* of the aura is created by thought, the *colour* by feeling. As in a picture, the two are inseparable except in theory. In an engineering drawing, form predominates, but there is of necessity a small modicum of colour too, while even the patches of colour in an impressionistic picture must of necessity have some kind of shape.

Feelings, or emotions, show in the aura in many ways. But the main features of the response are: an expansion or contraction, according to whether the feeling is one of outgoing or withdrawal; an increased or decreased brilliancy; and the production of the particular patterns and predominant colours associated with different feelings. The suggestion of an angry person 'seeing red' is typical of the latter characteristic, for the aura becomes suffused with clouds of red colouring while the intensity of the emotion lasts. When a man sees his favourite dog, his aura expands and a glow of affection lights it, but when the dog growls at a person who is afraid of him, that person's aura shrinks and becomes grey, its ordinary colours being dimmed by his nervousness.

An emotion is seldom pure, being almost invariably mixed with some contrasting or contradictory quality. Our attitude to a thing or a person is usually predominantly one thing, but is tinged with another. 'I like Mary, but she bores me.' 'My charwoman is a fool and irritates me beyond measure, but I am sorry for her.' I cannot easily say just where I stop liking Mary and become bored, or stop being annoyed with Mrs. Wiggins and become sorry. The visual description by clairvoyants coincides with what is known to psychologists of the feeling nature.

When we really think, the matter is somewhat different. The best compliment we can pay in this direction is to say of a person that he is a clear thinker: his thoughts are concise, sharp, orderly. Moreover, we like people to be unprejudiced. That is, we like to have a problem considered on its merits and without emotional bias, because the latter distorts and blurs the clarity of the thought-train. In a sense, therefore, thought and feeling are in marked contrast to one another, sometimes indeed, antagonistic, as when the emotional heart dictates one course of action and the intellectual head prescribes another.

The best type of thought results in clear-cut, sharp-edged, well-focused forms, whereas emotion is essentially open and fluidic. The active intellectual aura is like the screen in a cinematograph. The figures on it are generated by the self, as thinker, and projected on to this screen. A thinker following a concise train of thought produces a series of pictures or diagrams which move just as the film picture does, perhaps pausing, as when the film is stopped, so that a more careful examination can be given to a particular point. Thought about concrete things produces images more or less like that thing, according to the accuracy of the thinker's knowledge. The more abstract the ideas, the more the images are likely to be geometrical or symbolical in design. An architect designing a house creates that house in thought-material within his mental aura, and in his plans draws what he sees within himself. At first, his conception of the house may be vague; likewise his thought-form. He scraps the idea, thereby breaking up his original form. He begins again, and, having visualized clearly what he wants, he holds the form in his aura until he has done with it. The lunch gong goes, and he puts his thought aside—whereupon it thins out and disappears, like the Cheshire Cat. Later, he returns to his ideas, and the forms reappear as soon as he begins to work on them. Possibly during lunch his unconscious mind has been at work on the design, modifying the form, so that it now contains alterations and embellishments.

As one would expect, the same thing applies to any process involving thought, not only to such simple visual examples as those given. A written article, a piece of music, a poem, a diplomatic scheme, all show similar phenomena and can equally well be seen and described in terms of design.

As we know only too well, few people are really capable of clear thought, partly because most thinking runs concurrently with an emotional-, or feeling-train, and partly because so few people are able to conceive a clear idea of anything. Looked at from the thought-world, the man-in-the-street's idea of a house would probably evoke immediate condemnation from the Borough Surveyor, because the roof might be askew, the walls shaky, and the back of the house unthought-of and therefore non-existent. The same often applies to one's political and religious views; they may be as vague as one's thoughts about oneself or about other people, and one's mental aura is consequently apt to contain a flowing series or more or less ill-formed shapes which represent the ghosts of undefined ideas.

Not only is there very little pure thought, but almost all ordinary thought is coloured by feeling, just as most feelings cluster round some nucleus of an idea. The result is a compound of thought and feeling. The more feeling there is mixed up with the idea of an object, the less definite is the shape of that idea. The more forceful the thought, the clearer the form appears, the feeling-colour being subsidiary to the form.

The effect of training and habit is a tendency for relatively fixed sequences to form in the aura, so that the patterns corresponding to the habitual train of thought follow each other in regular order. The whole process is frequently unconscious and works like any other automatic routine followed in matters of daily life. In the mental aura of a merchant receiving an offer of goods there would be a series of forms corresponding to his habit of going step by step through the process of considering the nature of the goods, their quality, the reputation of the firm making the offer, the price of purchase, the price of resale, etc.

Besides the general configuration of the aura and the way it behaves, there is the effect of its behaviour upon physical consciousness. The physical reaction may be a purely unconscious one—a physiological change such as a fall in blood pressure or a rise in muscular tension or nausea—or it may be registered as 'I feel annoyed', 'I see the idea'—which are expressions of psychological states—or 'I feel depression creeping into the room despite my happiness at it being a sunny day'—which may express perception of external psychic conditions. The chakras, or psychic centres, seem to extend throughout the depth of the aura and are in reality coexistent at all three levels. It is by means of these delicate psychic organs that the various parts of the psychic structure are interconnected, just as the psyche in general is linked by them to the physical organism. For that reason, it is through the chakras that physical reactions occur in response to happenings at the emotional and intellectual levels of consciousness.

It should be noted, however, that the reactions of one level do not travel quite unhampered from one level to another, because between each level there appears to be a protective mechanism similar to the protective web described as covering the mouth of the etheric chakra. This acts as a filter and prevents the uninterrupted and unselected flow of impacts from the outer world indiscriminately invading the personality. Were the last to happen, there would be tumultuous upheavals, leading possibly to insanity, and such as characterize what Jung aptly describes as psychic invasions from the collective unconscious.

Incidentally, it should be understood that these finely

differentiated levels do not become immediately apparent to the ordinary clairvoyant. To be able to see them separately calls for a great deal of training. The clairvoyant must be able to shift his vision up and down the scale, from one level to the next, without losing continuity, in much the same way that we can train the eye to run along a road to the horizon instead of leaping from a near to a distant object.

CHAPTER VI

Common Psychic Conditions

The behaviour of the physical body is obvious: it is easy for us to observe how it acts and reacts, even if we do not clearly know why it does so in a particular way when confronted with certain conditions. The general principle, however, is that such behaviour is conditioned by feelings of attraction or of repulsion, under which every emotion can be listed. The body reaches or moves towards what attracts it, away from what repels it. These movements express in a general rule the reaction of every living organism to the material world about it.

It is only natural that the same rules should apply to the psychic worlds. And, since the aura, or psychic body, is also a living organism—or, rather, part of a living organism—it, too, follows the principle of movement towards a thing it likes and away from what it dislikes. Not only does a person *feel* relaxed, expansive, at ease, in a congenial atmosphere, but clairvoyance shows that his aura *is* actually eased out and wider than if he were strained, tense, or frightened. In the latter condition, the aura appears to retreat from the unpleasant circumstances and actually makes itself as small as it can, shutting up like a sea anemone at low tide, in its effort both to escape and to isolate itself from its surroundings. That is, the change of *subjective* feelings, or psychological condition, of a person, is seen by clairvoyants as *objective* movements of the psychic body in terms of space and size.

COMMON PSYCHIC CONDITIONS

It is a false idea to think that if we say we feel 'blue and depressed' we are merely using a metaphor, and expressing a physiological condition of depression in words having no reality in objective fact. On the contrary, to clairvoyant investigators, many phrases in common speech appear to be not metaphor and imagery, but to be based on intuitions of actual happenings in the aura of the person described. The psychic body of a person who is described as vivid, dull, grey, green with envy, glowing with love, filled with fiery devotion, or 'gone to pieces', actually appears like this to clairvoyant sight, as does one who 'lives in her shell' and has a cramped little aura with a hard, protective carapace in which she lives like a clock in a glass case.

Naturally, it may be argued that the clairvoyant only sees these things because they are suggested by the phrase which is used to describe a particular person's mood. This may be so in some cases. But if it were always so, one would need to explain why it is that there are many times when one feels a condition first, and only afterwards thinks of finding words to describe it: 'X was perfectly calm outwardly, but I knew he was seething like a stormy sea behind his mask,' 'I felt hurt and sore after meeting Y because, though he was politeness itself, when I mentioned Z to him he became as prickly as a sea-urchin.' Under such circumstances, a trained psychic would tend to confirm that the aura of X was really heaving and whirling with suppressed emotion, and that that of Y had changed from relative quiescence into an object with sharp needle-like forms in it, which actually *did* prick and hurt his companion's psychic organism. There is, besides, the common experience of meeting a person for the first time and knowing at once that that person dislikes one. In clairvoyant terms, the two auras have met and made contact, but instead

COMMON PSYCHIC CONDITIONS

of blending together they become resistant and instinctively
recoil from each other. There has been a real psychic colli-
sion, and it may happen that a hypersensitive person comes
away from such an encounter with a sense of shock, even
where no word has been spoken. In contrast to this, there
is the experience of going into a group of strangers and
suddenly feeling a sense of kinship with some other member of the group. This is, of course, helped if ideas have
been exchanged and it is clear that there is sympathy of
views, but it often happens without any lead from the
physical level. In this case the aura of each person glows
and expands towards the other, establishing a purely
psychic rapport which acts as a bridge between them. In
terms of music, the first case results in a discord due to
incompatible vibrations, whereas the second is a harmonious chord. In terms of colour, the first is a clash, the
second is a blend or a pleasing contrast.

In the physical world movements towards a desired object do not always reach the mark. But, in principle, one's
thoughts and feelings always reach the real object in
which one is interested. That is, though apparently a person may be interested in something outside himself, if the
true basic interest is self-centred and concerned as to how
that outside thing affects his own safety or well-being, the
wave of movement in the aura is a closed loop. It seems to
throw out a kind of filament which encircles that object
and returns to the person whence it originated. This can
be illustrated in the case of a woman looking at a dress in a
shop window: her reactions to it may be many and various,
and her aura behaves accordingly.

1. She sees the dress as an object beautiful in itself,
without thinking of it as one she wants to own: her aura
lights up and glows, and expands towards the dress with
pure aesthetic appreciation.

2. She sees and appreciates the dress and longs to possess it. Her aura lights up and expands as in the first instance, but the possessive desire throws out a tentacle which reaches out to the dress and acts like a hook trying to draw the garment mentally towards her.

3. She wants the dress, not because it is beautiful and suits her, but with a strong narcissistic feeling: she has a sense of her own beauty and feels that the dress will make her more attractive and call forth admiration of herself. In this case, it is not the dress she admires, but herself; the dress is merely a means of increasing her self-esteem. In this case the aura becomes her mirror, and into it she projects a thought-form of herself in the dress, and gets much pleasure and pride from contemplating that picture. As she is interested in herself alone, the whole movement takes place within the confines of her aura and never goes outside it at all.

4. She thinks she wants the dress, but she is not sure that it will suit her or that she can afford it. As she stands before the shop window her aura reaches out towards it while she is in the 'Yes' phase, then draws back while she hesitates, goes forward, again retreats, until she makes up her mind. She literally flickers. If she is of the kind who can never make a decision, and whose whole attitude to life is ambivalent and vacillating, the constant changes in her aura can become a disease and cause actual disintegration of the fabric. This then shows in physical ill health and in symptoms of neurosis familiar to psychologists.

An extraverted, exuberant person, whose whole energy is turned outwards and who is said to 'radiate vitality', does exactly this thing. His aura is like a fountain throwing spray in every direction, it radiates energy like a wireless transmitter. If his thoughts become formulated, more or less clear shapes are shot like rockets away from his aura. These either go off into space or else find their mark in the place or person to whom they are directed. As such people are often quite unselfconscious, their thoughts and feelings do not run in closed loops; they make no demand for themselves, and so do not receive anything back into themselves. But suppose something happens which quenches their enthusiasm, and they become self-conscious or afraid: the fountain dries up at once, the aura shrivels and loses its brilliancy, possibly deep depression sets in. Psychiatrists, incidentally, will recognize this as a picture corresponding to the cyclothymic type of Kretschmer. In insanity, the movement of the aura becomes quite detached from the control of the self and becomes automatic. The manic aura thus seethes and foams and throws off material, but this has no co-ordination or coherence and reflects the patient's jumble of talk and inconsequential behaviour. At the other end of the scale, the melancholic justifies his name by the deep grey-blackness of his aura, which becomes almost fixed and motionless, like a brooding black cloud. If he has an *idée fixe*, as many have, and repeats a hundred times an hour, 'I am dead' or 'I have sinned', the clairvoyant sees a faint repetitive movement occurring in some part of the aura, turning round and round on itself like a piece of clockwork mechanism.

Again, there was the case of a woman, well educated, well spoken, highly cultured, with an apparently charming and gracious personality. Her sad fate was that nobody ever liked to be long in close contact with her. Whatever house she was in was filled with her; and yet her outward behaviour was irreproachable: she was apparently neither an aggressive, dominant person nor the kind which focuses attention on itself by exaggerated self-effacement. But her personality was ubiquitous and pervaded the atmosphere of the house like the vibration of an aeroplane engine, even when she was shut away in her room. When she went out, a blessed silence seemed to fall. A clairvoyant description of her aura showed a good intellect but one quite without control over her powerful and unbalanced emotional nature. Her emotional aura was constantly surging and seething like an angry sea, filling the atmosphere around her with emotional spindrift. The whole condition was one of frustration. She had no interests that gave her emotional satisfaction.

Another person, a brilliant, witty, intuitive artist, yet had a deep vein of melancholy and pessimism which sapped the roots of his vitality, both physical and psychic. When this side of his personality was uppermost he would often succeed in depressing and tiring his best friends. His talk might be lively and clever, yet the atmosphere he carried with him depleted the energy and wilted the spirits of anybody within reach. His aura, when he be-came depressed, was exactly like a grey fog, colour and brightness fading out until he was, as he was often called, a veritable wet blanket.

A different picture concerns a maid in a house. Her em-ployers described her as 'clattering like a lot of empty tin cans'. Yet her physical movements were exceptionally light and gentle, and in direct contrast to the impression she gave people. Actually, she was a woman, probably of gypsy blood, who had had a very unhappy emotional life, and who was potentially a case of severe hysteria. In spite of her outward demeanour one felt that at any moment some unexpected spark might set her alight. Her aura gave the impression of many loose pieces rattling and colliding without rhyme or reason. There was no co-ordination or tranquillity in it.

These are pictures of psychological conditions, but they represent psychic facts and are consistent with the suggestion that the aura, or psyche, is an active organism. The physical body draws material from its environment according to its needs. It breathes and absorbs more or less oxygen, and it gives out carbon dioxide, water-vapour, and other chemical products, according to the state of its metabolism and whether it is active or at rest. The aura has a similar metabolism of its own kind. Some auras are like a catherine wheel, throwing off showers of sparks and ash, while others act in a centripetal way, sucking in and absorbing whatever satisfies their conscious or unconscious demands on life. In healthy physical life, the metabolism is balanced so that intake and output are the same. This principle also applies to a balanced psyche in which there is a genuine give-and-take between it and the people with whom it comes in contact.

These illustrations are given not simply as isolated phenomena, but because they are things which happen every day and everywhere. Unless we are of the tough-minded type, which either rides roughshod through life or lives in a psychic fortress without external contact, they affect us directly and sometimes profoundly, whether we are conscious of them or not. They are, however, the reactions of isolated people. Relationship of one person to another involves something more complicated. Reactions can be divided roughly into two main classes: one is due to an immediate or superficial mood or feeling, the other to fundamental temperament.

The reaction to a mood is a transitory and usually simple thing. The aura of the negative psychic behaves like blotting-paper and absorbs the prevailing atmosphere of the other person. If the psychic comes into a room where somebody is in a flood of strong feeling, he himself falls into gloom or becomes anxious by resonance to this feeling. The positive person may remain unaware of anything, or, if he should note the atmosphere, he remains unaffected and does not become involved. In fact, if he is strong enough, he may even steady or harmonize the disturbance by what he himself has to contribute from his own aura. This can be done without a word spoken, though an apt remark may act as a catalyst and start a resolution of the situation.

Temperament is a much deeper thing and is, moreover, complex. The reaction of one person to the mood of another is like the reaction between two single notes in music, which produce either concord or discord. The temperamental reaction is like that between chords played on instruments of different qualities and with different harmonics. These may or may not blend pleasantly. Where two people complement one another, the fringes of their respective auras flow easily together, interpenetrate and fuse, or withdraw and separate again, without strain. Each one has the effect of enhancing and expanding the other. In colloquial terms, they bring the best out of one another. This naturally results in creative relationship.

Children, as has already been said, are extremely sensitive to psychic impacts. Moreover, they are defenceless against them. Thus, an excited and exuberant person may cause a real psychic assault on the aura of a little child. It is not necessary for the excitement to have been directed at the child, nor for it to have been unpleasant and angry: if the victim has been within the radius of the blast he can be badly jarred and shaken. In one instance, a small boy invariably showed traces of his parents' quarrels on the following day, even though that quarrel had taken place out of earshot and in a part of the house remote from his nursery.

COMMON PSYCHIC CONDITIONS

Just as people carry and make their own atmosphere, so do places and things possess characteristic auras. These are, however, of a different order from those of living creatures. What we speak of as animate beings generate their atmosphere from within; it is a product of their own inner life, or soul. Inanimate matter has not a living self as a central focus of psychic energy, and its aura is not self-generated: it is built up by external factors. There is a dense physical structure with its counterpart made of etheric energy-matter. In inanimate objects it is this etheric film which acts as the basis around which the aura condenses. In the human being, the aura built round the central nucleus of the indwelling self is a radiation or emanation from that centre.

The etheric film becomes the basis upon which is imprinted a record of events and experience. Broadly speaking, the record is either one of a striking, clear-cut event or series of events, like the marks made on a stone with a mallet and chisel; or it may be of an indefinite nature, comparable to the effect of water washing over a rock and leaving it polished and worn by centuries of gentle friction. An accident, a murder, or some other catastrophic event highly charged with emotion, leaves a strong impression on a place. Equally deep, but different in quality, is the atmosphere built into an old house by generations of equable human occupation. The aura of the first is like the writing on a piece of paper which refers only to one event, while the other is like a tapestry of many-coloured threads weaving, crossing, and making a complex pattern of their own.

Frequently, the two factors combine. For instance, when a new cathedral is dedicated with great pomp and religious fervour, a certain current of thought and feeling is established. This is stimulated and kept going by the fact that thereafter the cathedral is used for one purpose—successive ceremonies, and worshippers each contribute a quota of energy which reinforces the original charge.

There is no limit to the amount which can be built into the aura of an object or place, and this is one reason why certain places feel rich with historical association and seem old and mature even to one who has no external knowledge of that history. A competent psychic will often unravel contrasting and even antipathetic phases of experience in the same place, as when an ancient church has in it at one level a feeling of deep and tranquil devotion and yet at another level there are traces of cruelty and fear due to the practices of the Inquisition.

Our response to atmosphere is based partly on temperament and partly on the sensitiveness of the receiving mechanism. One person is happy and at ease in a railway station, because the bustle and sense of excitement stimulate him. Another person is indifferent, and equally unaffected whether he be catching a train or sitting in his club. A third is battered and worn by the currents and eddies of constant movement, while a fourth, whose psychism is positive to such impacts, registers all the shift and change but does not allow it to distress him.

People who go to a museum respond differently, according to the purpose for which they go to it and the trend of their psychic make-up. From the psychic point of view, a museum is an interesting study. It is usually a conglomeration of all sorts and kinds of objects. These are classified according to history and subject but without any appreciation of their unseen qualities, that is, the mental and emotional associations which have become objectively attached to them. Many objects have become highly charged with an aura peculiar to the use to which they have been put. Such things as primitive fetishes often retain an aura of considerable power. Objects of this and other kinds are jumbled together, creating a chaos of unrelated psychic currents. It is as if each instrument in a large orchestra were blaring out individual notes, without any regard for the others.

In direct contrast to this would be a room devoted to one subject only, and in which the exhibits are not objects with a long history behind them, nor having a strong psychic charge from long use. Such a place as a Natural History or Geology room has a much smoother and less disturbed atmosphere than one given over to Archaeology, Ethnology, or a medley of collected *objets d'art*.

The negative psychic, who has no power of protecting himself from the cannonade of strong psychic vibrations impinging on his aura, is apt to become bewildered and fatigued after a short while in any collection of such objects. He feels he must either leave and get some fresh air, or he may wander through the galleries in a half-dazed condition in which he vaguely registers what he sees. Many people are struck by the curious, somnolent atmosphere in a museum, and the number of visitors who seem to be almost walking in their sleep, and this is probably the reason. In contrast to the casual visitor there is the student who sets out with a definite purpose in mind. His aura is braced and directed by his aim, and is consequently not in the flaccid, receptive condition of an aimless visitor. His absorption in his subject shields him from the assault and battery of warring psychic impacts.

Quite a different experience is a visit to a theatre. The theatre itself has a psychic atmosphere; the old theatre at Drury Lane, for instance, has an atmosphere very different from that of a modern building, and there is more justification than mere sentiment and historical continuity for producing certain types of plays there. The physical theatre has, as it were, certain permanent psychic stage sets of its own; and, as in a play action and scenery must correspond, so do certain plays fit in better than others with the permanent aura of the building. The drama relies much on the emotional reaction of its audience, and succeeds best when it appeals strongly to the feelings of the people. In the right conditions, the massed auras of the audience become exceptionally sensitive to the play of thought and emotion, and consequently the psychic background of the theatre itself is more important than it would be otherwise.

As each member of the audience arrives at a theatre, his aura is discrete, i.e. individual and separate. After a lapse of time, in which he sits in close proximity to other people, with the fringes of his aura overlapping and interpenetrating those of his neighbours, a gradual fusion takes place, so that a common psychic field is established. It is this composite aura which is at the root of crowd psychology. The individual becomes part of a group to which a collective name is given: an audience, a congreagtion, a mob, etc. The psychic field or general aura of the group is compounded from the greatest common measure of the thinking and feeling qualities that are there. In the theatre, the audience has a common focus of interest, the play on the stage. As the play proceeds, the aura becomes dynamic: it shifts and responds to every phase of the play, the colours changing with the rise and fall in the emotional content of the action, the field becoming taut at the critical dramatic moments, reflecting the development of the plot. The whole process rises to a peak at the moment of climax. The applause at the end shatters the common aura, which disintegrates into its normal components, restoring to each person some measure at least of the individuality he had temporarily lost. The intensity of the applause is at once a measure of the success of the play and of the degree to which the audience had merged themselves in it, and so of their need to restore themselves as self-contained individuals.

The behaviour of individuals within the psychic field of the theatre differs according to their psychological and psychic temperament. The primitive, 'all-or-none' psychic type is carried like driftwood on a stream. It is the behaviour of the water which governs the movement of the wood. The majority of people, however, tend to make a dual identification, one being psychic, the other psychological. The psychological aspect is where, as is usual, the onlooker identifies himself with some character in the play. This is often quite unconscious and becomes obvious only after a little introspection. At the same time there is a response to the psychic atmosphere. Often these work side by side and do not conflict; but there are cases where the psychic current runs in one direction, whereas the psychological current runs counter to it. Thus, in old-fashioned melodrama, hero and heroine are designed to meet with popular approval, and the villain with opprobrium. Hence anybody who, for one reason or another, identifies himself with the villain finds himself psychically caught in the popular current of emotional satisfaction when the hero overcomes the villain; yet his psychological desire is acutely hostile to this current. The result is a pull between the psychological and the psychic elements in the personality, and he may consequently feel discomfort, fatigue, and anxiety.

An interesting case of this conflict between psychic and psychological factors was that of a university woman who enjoyed the theatre but was sick every time she went. Analysis of her reactions showed that her enjoyment was purely intellectual, but that she felt herself emotionally swept away like a leaf in a gale. She remained powerless to control this until she realized she was pervaded by any strong atmosphere, anywhere, and that her psychic behaviour was negative. Her psychological make-up was such that she was afraid of emotion. She was able to control her own feelings and keep them rigidly in check, but those of others she could neither control nor keep outside herself. In this case, rather exceptionally, the psychological problem was allowed to remain unsolved, and yet she learned to handle the psychic difficulty. She had a trained and therefore powerful intellect and was able to use this intellect to detach herself from the ocean of feeling around her.

A dramatic critic, and a person who is aloof by temperament and lives psychically insulated, both enter the theatre with an attitude different from that of the average pleasure-seeker. Their auras never blend markedly with the others, although some degree of this occurs whether they like it or not. They tend to remain isolated, like an island in a lake. The attitude of the critic to the play is specialized, and consequently much more objective than that of the ordinary person: he does not identify himself. His judgment is therefore probably much more accurate than that of the general public. Yet, as we know, a play which the critics tear to shreds on literary and artistic grounds may run for years, simply because the playwright has succeeded in touching something in popular feeling and in 'putting it over' in such a way as brings about an easy psychic rapport between cast and audience. There is something satisfying to many people in being able to feel at one with a crowd and in being carried in its collective aura.

CHAPTER VII

Psychic Problems

It is well known that a person with a healthy mind and good physical health is largely immune to disease, whereas a negative, frightened, weakly person catches anything within reach. The same applies to the psychic world: a balanced, positive person keeps psychic atmospheres and miasmas outside himself, while a negative one tends to be invaded and deeply influenced by what takes place in the psychic world about him.

Just as physical temperament and capacity vary with each individual, so there are obvious inequalities of psychic make-up. These are congenital and intrinsic to the person: the individual is born what he is, and contains within himself a psychic mechanism with greater or lesser potentiality, and more particularly adapted to one line of activity or another. In some, a particular faculty such as clairvoyance or clairaudience, and the corresponding psychic channels, function normally from birth, just as the physical eye is active from the first. This is particularly evident in tiny children, for one may be highly reactive to psychic environment whereas another is oblivious to it.

Outside factors similarly vary. One child is born into an easy environment in which all is done for his education, while another may be in an atmosphere which is detrimental to his particular type. The first will be largely guarded from shocks to the delicate psychic mechanism, while the other will receive repeated assaults which are probably quite unrecognized by those around him, who fail to understand the reason for the child's exaggerated reactions. One person, for instance, remembered at the age of five or so, standing sobbing in the middle of every happy children's party to which she was taken, and being quite unable to make anybody understand what was the matter. She realized later in life how psychically sensitive she was, and saw that the other children's excitement and emotional activity had been objective to her: it looked and felt like a heaving sea with which she was unable to contend. She said she felt like a cork being tossed from wave to wave, so that she became increasingly confused and frightened. When she was rescued and taken to a corner to sit among grown-ups she felt that the rough sea no longer beat on her, and she was able to hold on to the stabilizing atmosphere of the adults and enjoy the party, no longer from inside, but as an onlooker. Many incidents of the same kind resulted in two things: one of these was a psychological fear and repression of her own emotions, the second a loathing and distrust of the psychic impact of other people's feelings.

In contrast to this, another small child was born with the capacity to see objectively both the physical and psychic worlds. Because the psychic vision was so natural, habitual, and positive, she was never frightened or bewildered by any of the things she saw in the superphysical world, and in consequence suffered no psychological injury or distress from her sensitivity.

In a case like the first, the psychological approach only deals partially with the problem. While it covers the fear of emotion in the child's own mind, it does not usually deal with the purely objective psychic percepts of the extra-senses unless they are recognized by both psychologist and patient for what they are. In psychotherapy, no difficulty is finally disposed of until a real and factual explanation has been found for it. To consider a subjective symbol as an objective phenomenon, or a psychic object as a subjective symbol, is to fail to understand the real meaning of each and to leave something untouched and therefore unresolved.

The fundamental difference between a hypersensitive and vulnerable person and one who, though sensitive, is immune from shock and injury, lies in the character of the etheric bridge-mechanism. Earlier in this book, this has been described as a complex field of energy. Where the streams of energy flow smoothly, without break or disturbance, and where their strength is maintained in a steady circulation of vitality, the etheric mesh is well-knit and resilient and provides protection to the individual from injury or contagion. Moreover, should any injury occur, it is quickly healed. At the physical level, such a person is largely immune from infection and contagious disease. At the psychic, there is also a certain robustness which saves him from psychic invasion and protects him from morbid sensitiveness to environment. He may, for instance, be in a room full of depression, or with a person deep in gloom, but he does not easily fall a prey to it, even if he should be well aware of it.

At the other end of the scale is the person whose stream of energy is choked. The channels in which it flows fall slack like a canvas hose when the water-pressure is low, and the tone of the whole mechanism is poor. The consequence is loss of vitality by leakage. The very fact that the pressure is low allows of such leakage, whereas the greater the pressure of vital energy the less permeable and the more continent the fabric becomes. A loose-knit etheric organism is largely defenceless against microbic infection, the action of drugs and anaesthetics which may cause symptoms of chronic poisoning, and against the assault of psychic impacts.

Good physical conditions do not necessarily entail a good psychic atmosphere: the most hygienic and the cleanest slaughter-house remains filled with the fear of the animals brought into it; and gladiator shows—whether in classical times or in their modern versions of prize-fights and all-in wrestling—appealing as they do to the aggressive and cruel sides of human nature—leave an atmosphere which remains long after the events which created it. Sometimes, in fact, the atmosphere of a place is far from simple, and has many layers in it. These can be sorted out and distinguished by the trained sensitive. Places dedicated to music, for instance, have a certain atmosphere in them; but if the hall be used also for meetings of political parties or for staging boxing matches, substrata of quite incongruous elements are built into the basic aura. On the other hand a hospital ward, physically cheerful, spotless, and carefully disinfected, is often psychically full of fear, pain, and distress, as well as of the atmosphere of sympathy and goodwill of the staff towards the sick.

Individual people going to such places tend to respond to the levels of the psychic atmosphere which touch some similar psychological material in themselves, and they may remain quite unaffected by the rest. Thus, a real devotee may be untouched by, and unaware of, the traces of Inquisitorial cruelty in an old church, while to another kind of person the atmosphere of the Colosseum in Rome suggests exhilaration and excitement rather than horror and dismay.

If, on the other hand, a complex atmosphere such as we have described touches on conflicting elements in the character of a person, or rouses in him some strong emotion or passion of which he is ashamed, it tends to reinforce and light up his psychological difficulties. Indeed, owing to the resonance between the psychic atmosphere and his psychological problems, latent conflicts may become active, and those previously mild may become violent and distressing. Moreover, confusion may occur even in a person who is self-aware, between the external psychic atmosphere and the contents of his own aura. He does not know how much of his trouble is due to his unresolved psychological material and how much is caused by an invasion of himself from outside.

It is well to realize also that, though we have spoken repeatedly of positive and negative psychism, there are as yet no such people as completely positive psychics—though there are plenty who are almost entirely negative. Even the best-trained person to-day has both positive and negative phases, as witnessed by moods and temperament: no man is a hero to his own valet for the simple reason that his intimates soon discover the weak spots even in the person whose public behaviour is always of the boldest and most positive. And, like the rest of the world, even the highly-skilled psychic has his heel of Achilles. At best, it is only a heel which is vulnerable; at worst, the whole body. Nevertheless, the principle stands, that positive psychism is objective and clear-cut, and negative psychism is confused and entangled with subjective psychological processes. The observations of the first reflect that quality of objectivity, and have that ring of truth, which satisfies the critical intellect, even if what is reported cannot be accepted as positively proved: but the second one will not stand up to critical analysis, even though there may be a quantum of truth diffused through masses of inchoate and unfocused—though possibly plausible—material.

A really civilized person has a balanced mind in which

all the various functions are approximately on the same level and have the same quality; in theory, no part of his personality is left behind so that it functions at a primitive level. If it should happen that some part of it is allowed to remain undeveloped, it may cause neurotic symptoms to occur. These symptoms can always be analysed out as evidence of primitive, childish traits of a kind which do not fit in with the general tenor of the rest of the life of the individual. Psychological re-education sets out to bring these childish levels into the light of consciousness, where, under the guidance of the intellect, they can be trained and adapted so that they are accepted as part of the make-up of the personality as a whole. In this process the primitive levels become changed and the savage in oneself becomes a civilized and useful member of the community of one's mind: before that, he either lived outside it and was a menace, or else inside it and was a nuisance.

If the psychic faculties in an otherwise well-integrated person are left in their primitive, negative form, they remain as slum-makers and disturbers of the peace. This is because they are out of reach of the intellect, which defines them and makes them work clearly and objectively. The result is confusion: there is no clear demarcation as to which of the images reaching the light of consciousness do so as a result of the psychic faculties perceiving things outside the mind, and what are the products of the mind itself—i.e. what are images of external objects and what are images self-generated within the mind. The condition, in short, is the same as that in the mind of a young baby where, as is well known to psychologists, he cannot yet differentiate between occurrences outside and inside his body, even at the dense physical level.

It is not remarkable, therefore, if it is found in practice that in many cases psychological states have a direct repercussion into the psychic receptive mechanism, as well as vice versa. This, moreover, accords with the principles discussed in describing the etheric bridge and its specific centres, or sense-organs. A bad psychological state may produce in the psychic organism a condition of strain or tension which makes of it a mechanism particularly prone to receive more or less severe shocks from psychic impacts.

This over-sensitiveness may be part of a general tendency to exaggerated reactions to both physical and psychic conditions. There are people on whom small quantities of certain foods or drugs produce a most violent effect, and who also give a response out of all proportion to noise, touch, or light; they become hysterical under psychological stress, and are completely overwhelmed by psychic atmospheres. This type is one which is known in medicine as hysterical, but the name does not give any real indication of the basic cause. The cause is actually somewhere in the subjective region of the individual, and is a lack of integration of the personality. But it is a far more difficult matter to explain why this lack of integration manifests in this particular manner and not in some other way.

Other forms of the same type of trouble are more localized. One may have a person who is allergic to certain foods, or one who is over-sensitive to certain psychological stresses only. In such people, psychic shocks may occur, and sometimes very easily, from some particular and individual cause. They are negative, and consequently open to sudden psychic invasion from outside themselves when a particularly sensitive shock-receiving mechanism is stimulated. For instance, a sudden storm of anger may arise in their immediate neighbourhood between two people who are complete strangers to them. Where people are open to this particular impact, the concussion of the anger so affects the solar plexus chakra that they may either identify themselves with the situation and become violently angry, or else it may have a physical reaction such as making them feel sick or, in serious cases, bring out symptoms exactly like those from physical shock. In all cases, the victims will be found to have similar material within their own psyche to that which caused the shock: a person cannot be shocked by anger or dragged down by gloom unless anger and gloom exist somewhere inside himself. This fact makes it difficult, in most cases, to distinguish between psychological and psychic reactions. In fact, the majority are a mixture of external psychic and internal psychological upheavals.

For an example of a purely psychic shock, we may take the case of a highly intelligent and sensitive woman who went into an empty room. She said afterwards that she felt as if she had walked into a battlefield and was being bombarded from all sides. Taken unawares, she became filled with panic and fled from the house without fulfilling her business there. Soon after, she was violently sick. She later telephoned to apologize for her behaviour, and learned that shortly before she went into the room it had been the scene of a first-class row. Had she been prepared, she could have steadied and braced her aura to encounter the onslaught of the violent emotional storm which was still active in the atmosphere, in just the same way as a person going out of a house on a windy day braces himself so as not to be knocked down by a sudden gust. This technique of dealing with psychic onslaught by adopting a positive attitude is legitimate and right. It is a means of self-protection, not of repression, and is consequently different from what is done when a person is faced with a psychological problem and raises defences so as not to have to face it. In the first case, the defence is against invasion from outside; in the second, it is a refusal to deal with conflicting material in oneself. In the first case, it is prevention of difficulties which need never arise; in the second, an evasion from an unsolved problem which already exists and needs to be dealt with.

In contrast to this experience, let us suppose that somebody receives an unpleasant letter from a solicitor, sent at the request of a neighbour who had always seemed friendly. The solicitor would have no grievance and would write without personal feeling, so that his letter would not be psychically charged with any animosity. Nevertheless, the recipient gets a shock. There is, however, no direct external psychic impact of anger, but the person feels that he has been deceived by the neighbour, or else that he himself has behaved so as to annoy him, and he blames himself for his own stupidity. The shock, in this case, is purely psychological and is due to the unexpectedness of what has happened.

A typical example, where mixed psychological and psychic material is confused, occurred when a person received a letter from a troublesome business colleague. He knew from the handwriting on the envelope that the contents would be controversial, and was prepared for this. On reading the letter, he was nevertheless badly startled by what he felt to be a venomous and uncalled-for attack. He put the letter aside for some days, then re-read it, carefully analysing both its actual wording, its psychic feeling, and his own reactions. The wording was controversial but harmless; but behind it he felt there lay an undoubted psychic atmosphere of violent anger and animosity. This was later proved to be correct. The shock on first reading the letter was due to unresolved psychological conflicts within the recipient's own mind, which were aroused by— and subsequently analysed in terms of—the letter and its writer. But the impact was due, not to external and visible things, but to the psychic atmosphere which was caused by the invisible and still hidden anger of the writer.

Serious psychic shock leads to a condition known as *psychic repercussion*. This is a phenomenon which results from the exaggerated response of a chakra. We have already described how these organs react to stimuli. Like the physical organs, they have a certain normal range of reaction beyond which they cannot go without injury. A muscle overworked or overstretched loses its power of response; the eye becomes blinded or dazzled by over-bright light; the ear 'buzzes' after being too long in loud noise. Similarly, a chakra can be injured by over-activity, and especially by a sudden and violent reaction.

The psychological reaction to a condition which results in shock is one of an emotional reaching-out towards the object which causes the shock. This is followed by a violent recoil away from the object. The whole aura of the victim springs into violent activity reflecting the psychological stages: first an expansion and enlargement, then a sudden contraction. This is shown in individual chakras by parallel actions: the outer end of the chakra leaps outwards, so that the whole organ becomes stretched and consequently longer and thinner than is normal. The nearest analogy is that of stretching a piece of elastic. The recoil reverses the process, and the chakra behaves just as if the tense elastic were relaxed and allowed to snap back, repercussing towards its base. This sudden expansion and contraction, if it goes beyond the normal range, leads to a shocked condition of the whole chakra, which reflects the psychological state. The latter may be a kind of emotional paralysis and inability to feel anything about the object concerned. The root of the trouble lies in psychological identification between oneself and the object—a matter which is fully understood and explained in psychological textbooks.[1] Reacting through the psychic mechanism in the way we have described, the psyche thus injures the fabric of the bridge over which it plays. After this, the chakra remains out of commission either until the effect has worn off or, in more serious cases, until positive remedies have been applied. To clairvoyant sight, it may appear to have become tightly closed, in appearance something like a daisy at night, but with a strong, cramp-like grip; or it may have splayed out saucer-wise; or, thirdly, it may appear no longer as a cone, but as if one side had become folded over towards the other lip, like a battered gramophone horn. The cramped condition seems to associate with emotional anaesthesia, and results in functional physical disorders such as sickness, palpitation of the heart, and so on. The splayed-out state leaves the sufferer emotionally unstable, uncontrolled, and quite confused as to the difference between psychological material and psychic invasions from outside. The third, distorted, state seems to lead to a lack of clear focus, and to distorted cognitions such as one gets from looking into a distorting mirror.

In any of these conditions, the proper interplay of the streams of energy is impaired. In some instances the incoming and outgoing streams become, so to speak, short-circuited, in others they tend to be largely checked. In any case, confusion results, and, moreover, the physical health of the person may suffer. This, at first, is functional—i.e. digestive disturbances or low blood pressure when the solar plexus chakra is involved, headaches, loss of voice,

[1] Bernard Hart in *The Psychology of Insanity* explains psychological mechanisms very adequately. Much more about identification is to be found scattered throughout psycho-analytical and psycho-therapeutic literature of all kinds.

heart disturbances, etc., for the others. But, later, after prolonged malfunction, the disease may spread to the actual physical tissues and result in deterioration of them at the organic level.

The shock itself may come from a sudden psychic impact from without—such a thing as an explosion of anger in another person; or it may occur from a violent subjective upheaval such as the shock from a piece of bad news or sudden fear. But, in any event, it is unlikely that this kind of injury to a chakra can occur except when the psyche of the person concerned has been jolted into tempestuous activity. A person of calm emotions and poised mind will not suffer from shock, because his responses keep within healthy limits, and he does not react unduly to whatever takes place.

Reference to the relationship between the mind and the responsiveness of the chakras, in Chapter IV, shows how psychological maladjustments are the cause of one or the other chakras being particularly liable to shock. The mental state, in the solar plexus chakra, for instance, may be such that, instead of a well-balanced rhythm existing in it, with a firm and steady field between its two poles, emotional stresses, complexes, phobias, make the field over-tense. Consequently, just as an inflamed eye or a piece of congested skin is tender and easily hurt, the chakra becomes over-sensitized and over-responsive. It is no longer only a sense-organ, but a piece of ill-balanced mechanism which easily becomes shocked.

The cure for such cases lies in two directions: one is in loosening up and readjusting the chakra itself by means of coloured light, breathing exercises, and the like.[1] The other, and most fundamental, is to remove the cause of the original strain, i.e. readjustment and re-education of the

[1] See Appendix B.

patient's psychological life and of his attitude to the world.

There are many different types of etheric body, but each one corresponds directly to the psychological temperament of the individual, and is related to the kind of thinking and feeling exercised by him. For instance, a man with a sharp, clear hard-thinking intellect has a taut and well-toned etheric vehicle; but if his emotions are soft and pliable, and sentiment should suddenly well up and overthrow his logical structure, the etheric gives like a piece of material released from tension. Another example is that of a person who lives in her emotions and never imposes on them the control of the intellect. Her etheric body may be vital, but it is uncoordinated. It billows and bulges like a slack sail, so that there are bursts of physical and psychic energy, but they are unstable and impermanent, and the person is either at the top of her form or in the depths of misery. These people are often over-receptive of psychic impulses, have generally some degree of clairvoyance or clairaudience, but the interpretations of their perceptions are very unreliable because they are so much coloured by personal bias. This is typical of the natural-born medium, such as is often met in the séance room. These people are often unable and unwilling to recognize that amid their accounts of genuine psychic experiences there is even a likelihood that they have woven in psychological material arising solely from their own minds. A psychic of this type will often unconsciously pick up from the mind of a client a perfectly true picture of a dead relative. She then proceeds to give what purports to be a message from this relative. In point of fact, it frequently happens that the relative is not there at all in person, but that the psychic has taken the picture from the mind of the client and is quite unaware that she has done this: to her, the picture is an objective phenomenon, and she cannot distinguish between a thought image in the client's aura and an extraneous and living entity. Probably, the message then delivered will be a mixture of what the client would wish to be told and of the medium's own eagerness to give helpful advice according to her own personal lights and attitude. The psychological material of the psychic is so much mixed up with her true psychic perceptions that the result is an inextricable confusion of the two. The output of every psychic affords ample evidence of the personal factor, even when the psychic work is relatively objective and positive.

Every child is born with a congenital pattern of physical make-up—fair hair, blue eyes, and a snub nose—and these persist. He cannot radically alter this structure, though within limits he can vary the expression of his face. The etheric field is also conditioned from the first, but the range over which alterations can take place is very much greater than is the case with the dense physical. The substance of the etheric body is far more subtle and malleable, and is influenced so directly by thought and feeling that it is possible to transform the psychic temperament into a pattern almost entirely different from that with which one is born. An example of this is that of a boy born with an etheric field so inchoate and plastic that from an early age he was the prey of discarnate entities who made use of him and frightened him severely by their pranks. They withdrew from him enough of the etheric material known as ectoplasm to play poltergeist tricks on him: articles moved about the room, crockery was broken, and, night after night, his beclothes were pulled off. At adolescence the child fell into the hands of people interested in psychical research, and he became a materializing medium, although he always felt a resistance to allowing himself to be used in this way. Later, he met psychically-educated people who explained that this uncontrolled psychic life need not continue, and that by a process of re-education he could transfer his negative capacities into positive faculties. This was a long and laborious process, but he succeeded to such an extent that, instead of giving trance addresses, he gave excellent and well-planned lectures under normal conditions, and instead of being a puppet at the mercy of discarnate entities he became a competent and self-directed research worker.

This case is one in which the psychic pattern showed in an exaggerated way from birth. There are many other cases in which the pattern never obtrudes itself or enters the conscious field at all throughout life. But there is a third type of case in which some experience wakes up a dormant possibility and brings it suddenly and violently into activity. The external impact may be slight, but it awakens a sleeping seed or potentiality, and the reaction is out of all proportion to the stimulus. This is because the seed has in it some primitive energy, lying latent and, as we know, primitive reactions tend to be 'all-or-none' and explosive, not gentle and measured. Such seeds are not necessarily connected with psychic faculty, but in certain cases may be strongly imbued with it. The mechanism is somewhat similar to that of the 'nuclear incident' known in psycho-therapy. In the latter, some event occurs in early life, in which the self momentarily loses control over an emotional situation. The fear caused by this loss of control, and the sense that one is on the edge of disaster, lead to the self taking a convulsive and repressive grip of the situation which it cannot thereafter relinquish until the incident is brought back into consciousness and the situation freely resolved. The seed, however, cannot be analysed in terms of childish memories: it is apparently there when the child is born, and is a part of his congenital pat-

tern. When aroused, it shows as a sudden, violent and uncontrollable reaction to a comparatively simple experience.

A girl of fifteen or sixteen, who was a first-class swim-
mer, and was quite at home in the water, was suddenly
pushed into the deep end of a swimming bath. In spite of
her competence, and knowing that she was really quite
safe, panic seized her as she went under the surface. Then,
in her own words, a tiny wheel began to whirl in her head,
and she saw pictures of what her family at home were doing. The startling thing was that when she got home she
found that what she had seen had actually been happening
at the time she saw it. Moreover, she remained consistently
clairvoyant for five or six years after this event, when the
faculty suddenly closed down again. She was much
troubled about this because she then felt that she had lost
something so vivid and valuable that life was incomplete
without it. A point which cannot easily be explained, is
that though the patient had had a hectic life, full of shocks
of all kinds, it needed this particular blow to stimulate
her latent clairvoyance.

The patient nevertheless thereafter acquired an unusual
sense of touch which went well beyond the physical range.
For instance, she was able to tell blindfold, by holding her
hand several inches away, whether material were smooth
or rough, velvet or silk, and so on. She was also highly
sensitive to atmosphere, whether of people or objects.
When she accepted the fact that this was a good substitute
for direct clairvoyance, she was satisfied. Her clairvoyance
had been limited to immediate knowledge of things happening at a distance, but her touch-sensitivity gave her a
range in another dimension—i.e. she was able to sense the
past history of things, to enter the atmosphere of the
times to which they belonged, and to make that history
alive and vivid to herself and others.

Another instance shows the complexity which arises from problems which are psychological in the sense that they originate from a negative attitude of mind in the individual, but eventually manifest in symptoms which are primarily psychic. This case was doubtless a serious one from the first, but the many kinds of treatment she was given served chiefly to make the difficulties worse and more complicated than they originally were. This was not only because they failed to touch the prime cause, so that the patient felt that nobody could help her, but also because the drugs and physical methods used were in themselves harmful to a patient who possessed such a psychic mechanism as hers. The patient was a woman in the early thirties exhibiting all the signs and symptoms of hysteria. When first seen, she was emotionally completely out of control, raving around the room in a state of high agitation and excitement. This had started as a result of a prolonged fast at the hands of a well-known exponent of unorthodox dietetics. However good these fasts may be for some people, this woman was one of the many for whom they are quite unsuited. She came out of the home in a state of physical collapse, with acute attacks of shaking and trembling, unable to speak without stammering. She was seen by neurologists, psychiatrists, and many others. At one time the suggestion was made that she had a cerebral tumour, but no positive evidence was forthcoming and she had the good fortune to escape an exploratory operation. Many other ideas were put forward, including that of certification as insane. The most accurate of these suggestions was that the patient was suffering from acute hysteria—as indeed she was. Finally she reached the hands of a physician who suspected that the cause of the hysteria itself was trouble which had a psychic origin, and felt that in such a case the narcotics with which she had been freely dosed, were worse than useless, and in fact positively harmful. He had the good sense to call in somebody who was competent to investigate the case from this new angle. Psychic diagnosis showed that the patient was markedly mediumistic: in whatever room she was, and even in the presence of other people, there was constant noise from psychic raps and loud crashes, as if the furniture were being struck with a heavy stick. Moreover, she could not bear to be touched even by her clothes, because her skin was so exaggeratedly sensitive that she felt acute pain on the slightest contact, and livid weals appeared. If she picked up an object that interested her, her mind became filled with vivid pictures of its history.

She was, nevertheless, a woman of excellent intellect. It was during the long fast that she lost control of her powerful emotional nature. This was because her etheric field was of the wrong type for this drastic treatment. It had consequently become devitalized and slack, and so, unstable and leaky. The web over the solar plexus centre was no longer protective and she was therefore open to every vibration about her. Sound was intensified and became an agony, light hurt her, and all her physical senses were out of control. On the psychic side she was the victim of all and every influence and could do nothing to protect herself in any direction.

Her history showed that she had always been very psychic. As a child she was constantly punished for 'telling lies' about things she saw, and she felt the bitter injustice of this. In her school years she would tell the fortunes of her mates for fun. At this stage, however, she got into trouble, not because she was accused of lying, but because her predictions had a way of coming true. The absurdity of the whole situation and the manner in which it was handled led her to repress the whole of her psychic nature, and it remained unconsidered and unconscious until, when the patient was weakened by starvation, it erupted volcanically into her conscious life, with distressing results. In this it behaved as any other repressed complex may do under such circumstances.

In the last stage of the illness she was constantly in a state of semi-trance and behaved in a manner inexplicable to people who had no knowledge of such conditions. From the psychological viewpoint she was carrying on the hysterical process by being in a state of dissociation in which she slipped constantly from being one personality into behaving and speaking as if she were another and quite different being.

The investigator who took over the case began by making the patient feel that here was somebody who understood her experiences and the real nature of the trouble. There was therefore a genuine point of contact.

She was told that there was no need for her troubles to go on, and that she was not suffering from an incurable disease. Nor was she mad. The combined but persevering application of a number of principles, each one in itself simple, gradually rebuilt the etheric structure and gave her psychic stability. These methods comprised deep breathing, the careful use of baths of light passed through selected filters, commonsense psychological advice, and training in simple mental exercises of positive affirmation. An important part of the treatment was avoidance of fatigue or strain. Diet had to be light and nutritious, and the patient was to have a hot drink at the very first sign of flagging. Drugs, alcohol, and over-hot baths, were rigidly forbidden. Satisfactory emotional outlets were gradually found, and the patient was given much friendly encouragement and moral support. After some weeks she began to return to a normal life, and her exaggerated psychic response died out, leaving a sensitive and responsive contact with life, but without the distress and suffering she had experienced before.

Another case, which at first sight seemed similar in some ways, was actually of a quite different nature. The first steadily worked away from the danger of being certified insane, but the second eventually had to spend some years in a mental home. This patient, a paranoiac[1] woman of fifty, complained that she was psychic, saw people out of their bodies, and heard voices. Significant to the psychologist is the fact that she said that she was haunted by her mother, from whom she could not escape. In this case the etheric body was intact but over-tense; the patient was in the state known as nervous tension, excitable, loquacious about the things she saw and heard. The mental-emotional aura above the head, instead of being smoothly ovoid, showed the clairvoyant a curious fissure like a cleft in a rock. Actually it was not so much a cleft as a rift due to the divergence of two currents of psychic energy. These currents would normally mingle and mix, but in such cases as these they separate out into conflicting and hostile material and repel one another, so that they turn away in opposite directions and leave a space between them which gives the appearance of a split. The psyche, in these cases, does not function as a single unit, and the appearance shown is always indicative of mental derangement of the sort classed by psychiatrists as schizophrenic, or split-minded, which includes such cases as this. The patient

[1] Paranoia is a mental disease characterized by delusions. The patient believes either that he is a very great person unrecognized or that he is being watched and persecuted. Frequently he is both: a king or a divine messenger who is being kept obscure by elaborate plots. In reality, both sides—i.e. king and persecutors—are conflicting aspects of the patient's own mind.

really had no contact with anything in the objective psychic world and outside her own aura, and the visions and voices were all within its confines. They only appeared external because the patient identified herself with one side of her psyche and relegated to the other the aspects of herself with which she was in conflict. It was as if she were looking from one room of her personality into another through a window in a partition and thinking that the things in that other room were really outside her house, instead of within it. As has been said, one important difference between a hallucination and a true psychic perception is that the first is within the person's own aura and the other entirely outside and independent of it.

As no alternative treatment was likely to be of any avail, an attempt was made to help the patient on lines somewhat similar to those of the previous case. She was taught to relax, to breathe correctly, and she was allowed to talk without contradiction or criticism about her experiences, while possible alternative explanations were lightly laid before her, to be accepted or rejected. She was a highly intelligent woman, and for a time she improved and the hallucinations disappeared. After some time, as the fundamental problem was always out of reach, she regressed into her old pattern, and she had to be taken care of for her own safety.

These two cases suggest that positive re-education is of primary importance when dealing with psychic cases. To sustain psychic stability, however, it is essential that the first steps should be combined with such study of his own mind as will make the patient understand the root of his difficulty and teach him to deal with it. Pronounced psychic problems are so individual that no hard-and-fast rules can be laid down for their treatment.

The psychological case, on the other hand, often needs

analysis and dissection first, followed by a positive synthesis. The constant difficulty is to know how to distinguish between the psychological and the psychic problem. Moreover, every case primarily psychic overlaps somewhere on to the psychological field, and many psychological cases run over on to the psychic. The dividing line is very subtle and it may be difficult to find where it lies.

A doctor once sent his sister-in-law for psychic investigation. Eighteen months previously she had had a major operation necessitating full anaesthesia. She had made a perfect recovery at the physical level, but she complained that ever since the operation she was not in proper contact with material life. She was, in her own words, 'not there'. The doctor was at first convinced that the condition was psychological, as it might well have been. But psychotherapy proved ineffective and wide of the mark. What had actually happened was that, on coming round from the anaesthetic, the etheric field had failed to return to its true alignment with the physical. Besides this, the solar plexus centre had remained clenched and tight, like a flower which had shut and could not open again. The condition was one of half-dissociation from material life, but the basis of this case was psychic and not psychological. The patient was of a decidedly psychic temperament, with a delicately poised and easily upset etheric organism. The anaesthetic appeared to have caused a deep, chronic poisoning of the etheric vehicle, and the patient was not sufficiently positive for the vital energies to clear the subtle poison out and to reactivate the mechanism. The etheric field consequently remained flabby and slack, and surrounded the dense physical body like an ill-fitting glove. In this case, as there was nothing seriously wrong in the psychological sphere, treatment was principally and directly of the etheric body. As the etheric cleaned up and its tone was restored, cure followed naturally and quickly.

This is an illustration of the subtle and lasting effect of anaesthetics and drugs on certain people. Physicians are often puzzled at the failure of vigorous patients to recover after anaesthesia. They complain of lassitude and lack of interest and energy, which is difficult to attribute to the shock of the surgical operation alone. Such people are often unexpectedly found to be over-susceptible to the effect of drugs. This does not usually show in a dramatic way, such as acute reaction to a small dose of a sleeping draught, but more commonly causes a prolonged loss of resiliency, and consequently a feeling of blunting of the keen edge of life. Such chronic dullness and retardation does not necessarily follow surgical anaesthesia only, but may arise after a period in which narcotics have been used, especially if these were of the barbitone group, which are nowadays so much and so lightly prescribed by physicians. The barbiturates have a particularly bad effect on certain people and especially on those of markedly psychic temperament, for they cause real deterioration of the etheric fabric, and this affects the personality as a whole. It is fortunate that the more perceptive psychiatrists are coming gradually to appreciate the dangers of some of the drugs used for sleeplessness or epilepsy. The results of mild drug-taking are often such that they make it for ever impossible to deal with the basic condition for which they are being given.

Any acute shock, physical, psychological, or psychic, may, as has been said, distort a healthy etheric mechanism. Where this mechanism is already debilitated, distortion or dislocation occurs all the more readily. Debility may be due to drugs, prolonged strain, fatigue, or malnutrition, and emotional unhappiness. Accompanying the general distortion there may be injury to a psychic centre. In particular, shock or strain tends in many people to disturb the balance and poise of the autonomic system by cramping up the solar plexus centre. When this condition is clairvoyantly observed, the etheric body is seen to be girded in by a belt of etheric material which is tightly drawn and tense, restricting the flow of vital energy. After a lapse of time such constriction impairs the metabolism and the digestion, with the result that more or less obscure digestive troubles can occur.

In another type of person the heart centre will be the one chiefly affected. This can result in 'tired heart' and other functional disturbances. If the throat centre is involved, loss of voice, asthma and thyroid troubles can ensue. In obstinate cases, after a lapse of time, the etheric stagnation caused by the inhibition of vitality leads on from a functional condition to actual tissue change and organic disease in the region affected.

There are many people who, throughout life, never feel in robust health. Often they are themselves puzzled as to the cause: they have no particular illness, and every doctor they see suggests some different reason, while every form of treatment fails ultimately to do more than give a temporary fillip to the patient. At one time it was the general fashion to attribute the cause to a subconscious retreat from life. This is often proved to be the case, but it is only one side of the picture. There remain a residue of cases in which the patient really and deeply wishes to live a healthy and vigorous life. At every turn he is baulked because his vitality fails him and he has attacks of extreme exhaustion. The blood pressure falls, he feels chilly, sometimes sick, and has a sense of general malaise. In such instances, the trouble often lies in a type of etheric field which is too much open to psychic and physical influences. A change of weather, loud noises, strong light, the presence of fidgety or restless people, on the one hand, and strong reactions to unexpressed moods in himself and others, all combine to upset the etheric mechanism and use up its energy. The patient is negatively psychic, and when he flags in the way described, his solar plexus centre loses its tone and co-ordination, flattening out limply, instead of being cupped like a flower-bell. In this condition it is over-responsive so that every sense-impact, physical or psychic, becomes exaggerated and painful. The etheric field as a whole loses its crisp texture and quality of radiation, becomes flaccid and grey, and falls in towards the contour of the dense physical body, looking like wisps of dirty grey gossamer chiffon. Until the etheric tone returns, the patient feels intensely tired and unable to bestir himself save with an immense effort. He feels that he must rest in a quiet place and let the world go hang. Paradoxically, if, instead of resting, the patient can make himself become active and, in particular, change his environment, it often happens that the new exterior psychic current will stimulate the depleted etheric and restore its tone. For instance, if he has been sitting and working indoors, a change into the garden results in his shaking off the fatigue, because of the psychic difference between the house and the outdoor world. The reverse applies equally well. What happens is that the over-receptive etheric mechanism picks up the new psychic atmosphere, which stimulates its flagging energies.

The sensitive psychic temperament has a habit of flagging because it is vulnerable to many more impacts than is normal, but this is also partly due to an underlying psychological attitude. This attitude is one of withdrawal from a life which is distressing and painful. The retreat is not necessarily associated with deep unconscious conflicts and complexes. To cure this condition, impersonal self-observation and awareness are needed. Then, if the patient chooses to assert himself and to come out and meet life, he must train himself in the laborious process of psychic re-education. The basic principle here is to develop a new pattern of thinking, rather than to churn up the old by too close an introspective analysis. Instead of being self-interested and self-pitying, and feeling himself to be unique and misunderstood, the patient has to see that his good and bad health lie in his own hands and that he alone is responsible. His mental approach to people and things directly affects his etheric organism, and if he can establish a positive attitude towards others he will gradually lose his fear of them. This breaks the vicious circle in which his very anxiety makes him vulnerable to the things he is anxious about. Learning to recognize and overcome his fears, and acquiring a sense that he is responsible for himself and can therefore do largely what he likes with himself, immediately provides him with the defences he needs.

This principle is clearly in direct contradiction to the principle underlying psychological analysis. The latter says, 'Let your fears come up so that you may analyse and understand them.' The psychic method is only similar in so far as it calls for self-awareness and for bringing matters into the conscious field. But, thereafter, while the psychologist says, 'Absorb and assimilate the fear and do not try to keep it out of your conscious field, learn to bring it up and deal constructively with it,' the psychic method is to make the patient aware not only of the problem but of the subtle mechanical happenings in the psyche, which are exactly on a par with faulty muscular contractions and lead to bad posture and stiff movement. In the psyche, tension and cramp, or over-relaxation, lead to lack of alignment and to distortion of the mechanism. To cure this involves, not a passive acceptance of the maladjustment, but a positive action to correct it, i.e. active therapeutic measures to re-educate the psychic organism. Fear causes the psychic mechanism to tighten and the solar plexus centre to become cramped. The psychologist's task is to help the patient to analyse the hidden roots of his fear. The psychic, however, teaches the patient to realize the tension in the mechanism, and how that tension weakens mental and emotional control. By direct methods of positive thought, breathing, etc., he tries to teach the patient how to steady and relax the mechanism directly, by imagination and intention, and thus to allow the vitality to flow freely once more. He does not necessarily touch the unconscious cause of the trouble, if there is one. The two methods are complementary.

This all goes to show that when one is confronted with complicated problems of health there are at least three angles from which the subject needs to be considered. There is the medical angle, which looks to the physical condition, hygiene, nutrition, sepsis, and so on. The psychological angle which is concerned with the mental attitude and with conflicts and complexes within the mind of the patient. The third, the psychic, which is concerned with the subtle fabric of the mind and the senses by which it contacts the external psychic world in which it lives; the etheric bridge, and the health, development, and activity of its psychic centres; the degree of the patient's awareness of psychic experience.

These three angles of the personality triangle are intimately related. But it is obvious that if the trouble really originates in one angle, to treat it as if it originated in one of the others can be at best only palliative, whereas at the worst it can be positively injurious.

There are as yet few if any means of giving scientific

proof that this third angle is important in any particular case. No unwilling person can be persuaded of it, yet there are many instances in which the experienced observer sees at once where the trouble lies. There are many cases in which the patient complains of troubles which the doctor knows to be purely psychological in origin. Yet if the doctor ventures to suggest that mental treatment is advisable and refuses the bottle of useless medicine the patient expects, the latter is apt to lose his faith in his physician. All the more do certain people resent the suggestion that uncontrolled extra-sensory faculties may be involved, since one is there treading on delicate and mysterious ground. Nevertheless, there are many such instances, especially among artists and others who habitually deal in subtleties and overtones which they find inseparable from their ordinary perception of life. These people instinctively and unconsciously accept the psychic approach, but may find themselves in difficulties simply because it is unconscious and not explicit. Their experience, however, is such that for them there will be nothing strange or far-fetched in the principles discussed above, even if they go far beyond anything of which they are as yet aware. Moreover, in these matter-of-fact days, many sensitive people are shy of letting on, even to themselves, that they see and feel things in apparently strange and unique ways. They thus tend to shut themselves up in a lonely little world of their own, which is psychologically unhealthy and frustrating. But they are not really alone in these experiences and difficulties: they are the lot of many, and perhaps especially of the intelligent and cultured people of to-day. Moreover, they can be explained and understood—but only when they are discussed and shared in an atmosphere of objective and critical discussion. In this way, in years to come, it may be that a body of psychic pathology may come into being which can be placed beside, and on a level with, what is already known of the pathology of the body and of the subjective aspects of the mind, so as to make a firm tripod of knowledge on which a new medicine can be built.

CHAPTER VIII

Nature and Ourselves

The primitive and the child perceive the psychic and the psychological worlds as one. They have not yet established the distinction between the self and the not-self which comes with the development of the intellect. The savage peoples the whole of Nature with spirits: rocks, rivers, trees, and winds are to him the abode of non-physical entities ranging from tiny fairies, gnomes, and goblins, to a hierarchy of powerful gods. With them he must keep on good terms or suffer the consequences. Out of these ideas, whether they be true or false, arise primitive animistic religion and all the rites and superstitions of primitive folk-lore.

According to certain schools of psychology, animism such as this is based on nothing more than a projection into the outer world of the contents of the savage's own mind. Consequently, the whole of folk-lore and of religion is said to represent simply an attempt to placate the parts of oneself of which one is afraid, and to encourage those of which one approves. The broom of science thus sweeps away, not only the cobwebs of superstition, but also the whole structure of religion and mythology around which they hang, and brings the Godhead tumbling down with the rest. Further, for the simple reason that there is a deep and urgent desire in man to believe in the existence of God, and in spirits and daemons, there are some who believe that this desire alone is enough to disprove their existence. For, they argue, if one *wants* to believe in a thing which cannot be seen and measured, one can be sure that the belief is false and childish. Freud, for instance, has taken the trouble to write a whole book in order to explain away religion of all sorts, whether transcendental or primitive, by reducing all its tenets to the terms of his own pan-sexual theories. This, no doubt, is a great *tour de force*, but is it anything more? And does it, in fact, invalidate religion?

In any case, the logic of materialism is poor. In the first place, the fact that man wants to believe in a God and in spirits does not prove that they do not exist. The comfort of being able to hold religious ideas certainly introduces a bias into the mind, and rightly makes the logical scientist chary of accepting such doctrines, but he knows that it does not automatically rule them out.

Besides, on the other side of the scale, there is a vast weight of belief that Nature is not wholly physical and material, but that it has psychic and spiritual counterparts which have a great influence on those who live in close contact with her. The wise scientist, moreover, recognizes that where beliefs of any kind are persistent and universal there is somewhere in them a kernel of fact and logical truth, even if the outer husks are childish and give rise to superstition and obscurantism.

Science does great service to humanity. It tells of the laws of physics and chemistry, and reduces the universe to an orderly plan. More and more we are learning to know where we are in relation to the forces of the cosmos. We can in some measure foretell the weather, we can prophesy the result of our actions because we know what energies will be unchained by them, and the direction they will take. We know that the aurora borealis is an electrical phenomenon involving so many millions of volts, and that it is not just a manifestation from a temperamental deity. It is true that we cannot control the aurora; but we can, ourselves, by a certain structure of wires and magnets, generate other electrical energies which we harness and use for our own ends. In short, man's scientific intellect is leading him on step by step to a conquest of the universe and to an enlargement of himself and his consciousness.

Indeed, it goes further than this. As the scientist grows in understanding, he finds unfolding before him a panorama of the cosmos which is awe-inspiring in its vastness. Because the scientific, orderly laws by which it is governed are at once so minute and perfect in every detail, yet conceived on so huge a scale, materialism fails. The scientist with vision finds himself faced with the conviction that there must be some transcendental intelligence in the universe, in which or in whom all scientific laws are embodied and within whose orbit the whole cosmos exists. In short, he has passed from science to mysticism and religious experience and has once more found and seen God—not a God of whims and temperamentalism, but a God who is a scientist, an engineer, an architect, and an artist. Eddington and Jeans in the sphere of astronomy, Jung in psychology, McTaggart in metaphysics, are only a few of the growing number who afford testimony of this.

But the world is not peopled with scientists, and among scientists there are few who have the insight to see more than a limited field. There are, however, others whose approach to life is less through the intellect and more through the feelings and the intuition: the artists, the poets, the dreamers, those who feel that the lower reaches of science are only too often destructive of the things they hold most dear. Many of these consider that the practical man's approach to Nature is a violation, that he sets out to conquer and enslave her by power and force of intellect.

To people with this attitude, Nature is full of life, and they feel that she deserves consideration and respect, that a proper relationship with her should take into account the rights of that life to its own expansion and development. Further, they feel—often rather confusedly—that the man who respects that life and approaches Nature in order to enlist her co-operation, seeing her as an ally rather than an enemy to be overcome, or a victim to be forced into subjection, is far more likely to achieve his ends than the man who ruthlessly tramples her down for an ephemeral and purely material benefit.

The scientist of limited outlook finds it easy to dub these people imaginative sentimentalists, and to say that they are merely projecting their childish fantasies on to the trees and clouds they call their friends. But these children are apt to remain obstinately unconverted and to cling to their intuitions, even when they are intelligent and clever people in other respects. Science, after all, has not even negative proof to offer that the beliefs they hold are false. Scientists may rightly say that there is no evidence that fairies, sylphs and undines haunt the woods and waves; but, if they are logical, they must also admit that, out of reach of the senses and of any scientific instrument yet devised—and each new telescope reveals new stars hitherto unseen—there may be many things undiscovered, and that consequently the old loves and beliefs of simple people may yet tell of objective realities and not only of subjective fantasies.

Science must, then, remain agnostic and sceptical—i.e. not-knowing, and doubtful, but open-minded—as to the existence of non-physical beings. It has a word of warning both for the one who desires to believe in their existence and the one who dogmatically asserts that he believes only in what he can see and measure by physical means.

NATURE AND OURSELVES

The psychic approach bears out both the scientist's and the artist's views. The universe is in truth one of law and order, where each thing has its place and conforms to certain rules; but there is no corner of it in which, behind the structure and the forms, there is not also teeming life. In some places, and at some levels, this life is an unconscious inchoate ocean of activity, or energy; but as one ascends to more advanced levels, this ocean gradually differentiates itself and parts separate off from the mass, assuming forms of increasing elaboration and refinement. Ultimately, these differentiated parts become self-conscious, and thereby acquire the beginnings of self-direction, of free will, and free choice.

This is to be seen in the physical sphere, where consciousness evolves together with differentiation of one individual from another, and with the complication and elaboration of the body. In the animal kingdom, for instance, it would be almost impossible to tell one amoeba from the many million others of the same species: they all look alike, and their behaviour is governed by the same simple instinctive urges. Nor could even the subtlest observation discover any difference in the intelligence and character of any one of them. The more primitive the animal, the more he is part of a mass, and the less individual he is.

As one rises in the scale of evolution, variations occur on an increasing scale, both in form and behaviour; the ocean of instinctive life splits up into separate droplets. Each of these becomes progressively more individualized as its experience increases, more conscious and self-directed and more able to choose between alternative courses of behaviour.

The same appears to occur in the psychic worlds. The creatures of that world seem to follow the same general

laws of evolution as do those in the physical, from unconscious, instinctive mass-behaviour up to levels of high
awareness and individuality.

Most people are not scientific, nor do they formulate
their ideas in words. Indeed, many are quite unconscious
of having either ideas or knowledge about the vital background to natural phenomena, even when they automatically act in accord with it. The life of the born countryman
centres round his intuitions about Nature, though if one
were to question him as to why he does or says certain
things he would be quite at a loss. Such people are quick
to sense the temperament and atmosphere of natural
objects and environments, and this is partly why the reputation of certain places grows so quickly and is so univer-
sally accepted by them. It is more than whimsicality which
makes them say of a certain tree that 'Her's not friendly'
or that a certain pond is 'A danged wicked place'. From
the psychic angle they seem to be instinctively responding
to the demands made by the hidden side of their environment.

Among more sophisticated people, if one speaks of a
certain tree as 'a real friend' or 'a beautiful person', somebody who loves that tree may say, 'I've always felt that but
did not know how to put it.' Then perhaps this seemingly
matter-of-fact person goes on to confide that he feels that
his roses have their own likes and dislikes and grow better
if he talks kindly to them, or he tells you that he thinks his
tomatoes did badly because he was in a bad mood when he
planted them, and they felt it.

A certain man who went to live in a house which had
beautiful trees in the garden was keenly aware of these
things, in spite of being an efficient business man. Among
the things he decided to do was to put his wireless aerial up
in a suitable tree. Before he did it, however, his daughter

remarked to him, 'That oak tree won't understand what the aerial is, and will be uncomfortable.' She expected him to laugh at her, but to her surprise he replied casually, 'That's all right; I've just been down the garden and explained to it what I'm going to do.'

A somewhat similar instance occurred when a person who had all her life seen clairvoyantly many natural creatures, was standing looking at a waterfall with an elderly friend. She mischievously said to him, 'Look at those undines in the spray!' He answered in a matter-of-fact way, 'Yes, they are having a good time. Look at that one just slipping over the edge.' She thought he was playing up to her but found that he was serious and knew as much about them as she did.

Unconscious acceptance of the fact that there is more in Nature than the eye can see also explains the difference between the country-lover and the country-hater. This is not merely a matter of contrast between muddy lanes and clean pavements, fresh *versus* soot-laden air, but of subtle response to the psychic difference between a man-made atmosphere and the less complicated and gentler rhythms of Nature.

A town produces a maelstrom of unseen vibrations, in which a vast network of mechanical systems vies with the concentrated human element in throwing off emanations, the confusion of which can produce psychic friction and disturbance. The psychic clamour of a big city, beating continuously on the aura, either stimulates and activates the individual, or else fatigues and confuses him. To some people who have become accustomed to it, this cacophony gives an apparent safety, while to others it is damaging.

The country, on the other hand, seems to the urban mind either flat and uninteresting because the accustomed stimulation is lacking, or frightening because its stillness permits the slow, inexorable instinctive urges, which man so often tries to repress and ignore, to rise to the surface of consciousness. At dusk, especially, such people are apt to become a prey to depression or fear, and to feel that they are being dragged down into haunted depths peopled by strange creatures of uncanny power. This is due to more than psychological suggestion. At sundown, there is an actual change of psychic current on the surface of the earth, and the negative psychic responds to the undertow of the countryside from which he is shielded when there is noise and bustle to keep him extraverted and busy.

In psychological practice, one frequently meets with people who tell how, as children, they were terrified at having to go into some part of a wood, or past a certain rock, or who felt a strong urge to throw themselves into some particular pool. This may be due to one or more of three distinct factors.

First, there is the purely psychological: association of ideas, such as the form suggested by the rock, which may look like some dragon or monster. Or it may be that the scene recalls some other place where a highly painful incident occurred.

Second, there may be a purely psychic atmosphere about the place, built up by the thoughts and feelings of human beings. A research worker was asked to investigate a so-called haunted room. The woman who lived in it, an unhappy creature, complained that something in the room constantly urged her to jump out of the window into the stone-flagged courtyard below. The investigator himself stood at the window and realized that it would be an ideal place for suicide, but he failed to discover any trace of haunting. He realized, however, that many people must have thought as he did, and had probably built up in the room an atmosphere of corresponding thought and feeling.

It was to this, and not to any haunting entity, that the lady responded. Her response was all the stronger because of her frustrated psychological life and her wish to escape from it. This atmosphere was psychic but man-made.

The third factor is where Nature alone creates the psychic atmosphere, and where the human element does not exist. There are remote parts of Dartmoor, for instance, where sensible people have found themselves seized with panic for no apparent reason except that the moor itself seemed hostile and sinister. It was as though it resented human intrusion. This is also felt in wild mountains, such as parts of the Alps. One wood may be physically dark and sombre, and yet be friendly, while a much lighter and sparser copse is hostile. Again, one may camp out on a deserted fell in Norway, and yet feel as if one were surrounded by busy living creatures. Such impressions as these have nothing to do with humanity and human thought: they are an integral part of those particular places and seem characteristic of the natural life in them. In some parts, as in wild mountain country, this life is very potent, and inspires fear from the fact that it is completely alien to and incompatible with humankind. There is nothing evil in it; it is merely life of another order, and to understand this and accept it as a fact in Nature removes the sense of menace by an unknown danger.

To recognize these unseen powers in Nature, and to realize that they cannot overwhelm or even invade us unless we allow or invite them to do so, is highly important to the negative psychic. It puts him in a position to withstand the impact of frightening and uncongenial intrusions which are only disturbing when he registers them without realizing that they have no fundamental relationship with himself.

All this may be of very little importance to the majority

of people. But there are many others who feel a secret and unexpressed affinity with Nature, and an inarticulate wish to be on more friendly and intimate terms with her. Some of these have 'green fingers', others can handle animals or are 'rare hands with bees', while there are others who seem to know everything about trees—except their botanical names and classifications. Where a person has a real knack for understanding and making sympathetic contact with any aspect of Nature, it is safe to say that there is a natural psychic affinity between the two. The good water diviner; the intuitive horticulturist who instinctively selects the stocks from which to evolve new varieties; the clever technician whose mind jumps to the solution of a mechanical problem: all of these have something in their make-up which creates a psychic rapport with the material with which they are working.

All these and many other things can be discovered by those who think seriously and yet sympathetically along these lines. The way of discovery, as has been said before, is to experiment for oneself, with an open mind, a backing of common sense, and a realization that tact is as much needed in approaching strange aspects of Nature as in approaching human strangers. One should not gate-crash into Nature's unseen world, or one may find that she resents it, just as human beings resent unwarranted and impertinent intrusion, and that she has a way of 'getting back' at one just as they have. But Nature offers a whole host of new and fascinating acquaintances, and even friends, if we set the right way about getting to know her.

CHAPTER IX

Perception, Fantasy, and Imagination

The first part of this book has been a study of the extra-sensory, or psychic, faculties, and has tried to show how these affect daily life. The need for doing this lay in the obscurity in which these faculties were plunged, and because psychological science has so far steered round them and considered them as anomalies rather than tackle them simply and honestly as part of common experience. Consequently, it seemed necessary to bring this particular aspect of the psyche strongly into relief. This may have made it seem as if it were something quite separate and distinct from the rest of the mental world. This is not so, and to see psychic perceptivity correctly it must be seen in relation to a whole. The mind has many departments, and all are equally important. The psychic faculties need to be allowed their proper place in mental activity, without being either exaggerated or ignored.

To recapitulate, perceptivity is one function, and physical, psychic and spiritual perception fade into and, in fact, overlap one another. It is impossible to say where one ends and the other begins. The borderline between physical and psychic can only be gauged by what part of the receptive mechanism is being used at any particular time. To change over from the use of physical to the use of psychic sense-organs is to carry on just the same psychological process through a different part of the mechanism: it is like turning the switch on a radio which makes it respond to short waves instead of to long. Moreover, as in radio, there is no sharp break between short and long waves, and it is quite possible for a set to pick up the same wavelength on both long and short wave tunings if the range of each is wide enough for them to overlap. The psychic sense is simply extensions of the physical—or vice versa, according to the point of view. In all cases, the language in which we perceive is that of the physical senses. We can say little of spiritual illumination: it has no language except that of paradox and contradiction.

If we are imaginative we give piquancy to a description by suggesting that a picture contains music, that music is pictorial or architectural. This way of combining impressions is known as 'apperception': the ability to bring together different aspects of an idea so as to create a fuller and deeper understanding of it. 'Don't you love that bit where the 'cellos go all soft and furry, like brown velvet?' asked a friend, listening to a particular part of a symphony. The description was admirable. But it suggested to the psychic that, in such cases, apperception may simply mean an unconscious combination of physical and psychic perceptions of the same thing, which thereby create a picture in relief instead of one on the flat.

The ability to perceive may be largely concentrated on the physical end of the scale, where psychic impacts cause reflex actions without being consciously perceived; or it may overlap on to both sides and take in a considerable amount of psychic ability as well as physical; while there are a few people who are highly perceptive at the psychic level, and who perceive very little of the physical world. The latter, of course, are always in trouble, and receive shocks from the physical world because they are so much out of touch with practical realities and ordinary affairs.

It does not follow, from the above, that the range of perception in any given person is continuous. Moreover, most people tend to excel in one direction and to be less good in another: there are, for instance, people who are primarily visual types, others auditory, and so on. Moreover, when a person is physically of the visual type he tends to be psychically clairvoyant rather than, as in the case of the auditory type, clairaudient, while the person who senses the physical world mostly through touch leans towards clairsentience and psychometry of objects at subtler levels.

Many people, of course, are not interested in anything more than perception: they prefer to take things as they perceive them and leave speculation to others. They belong to that half of humanity which William James has dubbed the tough-minded. They do not want change; they are content to take things as they are; they think speculation and progress are dangerous. They feel no urge to grow, and are content to travel in the grooves of old patterns of thought, feeling and action, and they resent, fear and resist anything which tends to break their routine. If circumstances should force them out of their old world and oblige them to change, they receive something of a shock, and possibly suffer breakdown and disaster. In contrast to these, there are the tender-minded: those who feel the urge to grow, to progress. They are the ones who are ever questing after new experience, new knowledge, both of themselves and of the universe; they are restless and experimental. The tough-minded are stable and reliable at best, dull and stodgy at the worst. The good type of the tender-minded is progressive and creative, the bad type unstable, unreliable, and erratic. In practice, every intelligent person has in himself some of the characteristics of both types, with a predominance, more or less strong, of one. And, naturally, both types are necessary to the community. The tough-minded, merely-perceptive type are its backbone and keep it from an amoeboid shapelessness. But dry bones never get anywhere unaided and are apt to crumble into dust.

The tender-minded often feel that perception, no matter how extensive and elaborate, no matter how much of the psychic is added to the physical end of the scale, really tells them very little of what they want to know. They may perceive through their psycho-physical senses the most interesting and enchanting things, yet they remain unsatisfied and frustrated. Perception, unaided by other mental functions, is a disappointment; it tells what things look like, but it fails utterly to tell what they are, or what is their true relationship to one another.

To the animal, all that matters is to know the appearance of things: when they have used their senses to perceive an object the blind, instinctive urges of nature do the rest, and lead them on to the satisfaction of those urges: if what they perceive is dangerous, instinct drives them to flight, if it is good to eat they seize it, and so on. The animal's goal is simply to satisfy his need to survive and reproduce, and with that he is content. Perceptivity is developed to serve that end and, so far as he is concerned, that end alone. In man it does the same. But man, in addition to working to survive and breed, wants to know the world just for the sake of knowing it. It is at this point that perceptivity soon fails him unless he uses it as a starting-point for other mental activities which are essentially human and which, as far as we know, do not exist at all in animals.

Perceptivity thus becomes only the first step in the acquisition of knowledge. It is an animal and instinctive function, and, like all other instinctive functions, it needs to be taken up and made into a part of the human personality as a whole. That is, it needs to be directed by higher aspects of the psyche and used for human and not purely animal ends.

Perceptivity appears to be the starting-point for two main paths of mental activity. These are, respectively, logical thought: the deductive and inductive, scientific method, which proceeds sequentially, step by step; and imagination, which goes in seven-league boots, disregarding the intervening miles of road by which logic travels.

Logic is a safe path for those whose way it is. Moreover, it is one well charted by philosophers. The way of imagination, however, is not so safe, nor is it so well understood. It is easy to lose one's way in this mode of airy travel and to come down at the wrong place. But it is not therefore to be despised. On the contrary, if imaginative travel be used together with the maps supplied by logic, it becomes a rapid and useful means of journeying from plain perception to wider fields of knowledge. It is only when the two become separated that we are apt to say imagination fails us and we find ourselves bewildered and at sea. What this means, is one of two things: that, in our imaginative flight, we have lost our place on the map we should be carrying with us, so that we do not know where we are; or else that, between us and the earth, the air is not clear, the atmosphere is clouded with emotion and desire.

When we thus lose our way, it is not really that imagination has failed us, but that we have allowed something to intervene between ourselves and common-sense reality. Two courses are then open to us: either to bring our imaginative aircraft down to earth and find out where we are, or to go on drifting blindly in the clouds without sense of direction or location. This is known as fantasy. To sum the matter up it may be said that logic travels by road, from step to step; imagination flies from point to point, with a sense of direction and by correct navigation which can be checked by means of the map which logic provides; whereas fantasy is mere joy-riding: a pleasant flight off the solid ground, among the clouds, but it brings one back to the same point as one started from.

This analogy supplies the key to a distinction between the imagination as a creative, forward-moving thing and its morbid manifestation, well known to psychologists. The difference is so great that it needs to be emphasized. To some psychologists it is clear, but to some it is not, and all imaginative flight is classed as unhealthy, without distinction between two processes which have only this in common: that they take place in the air and above the ground of material things.

Fantasy is not a healthy process, nor useful except in one way. This is if it is strictly under control and taken in moderate doses, so that it does not interfere with healthy and creative mental and physical activity. It is then a means of recreation: certain types of novels,[1] films, plays, and all the escape activities which we use to rest ourselves from the stresses of modern life, fall under the general heading of fantasy. The trouble begins when we get lost and cannot shut the book or come out of our daydreams and 'go to it' again.

Fantasy is the subject of much psychological discussion, and there is no need to enlarge on it further from this angle. But psychic observations suggest certain prin-

---

[1] It is well to realize that all fiction is not escape: when it has in it the quality which makes it a work of art, and is studied with understanding, it is not a retreat from reality, but a contact with reality in a different way and of a different kind from that made in outward activity.

ciples and pictures which, from a quite different aspect, confirm the ordinary psychological view. Moreover, these pictures help to clarify the distinction between fantasy and creative imagination.

Observed psychically, two main types of fantasy life can be described. In one the person feels himself to be a hero or a prince, and goes through life in that role. He is permanently an actor, and his life is conditioned by the part which he has assumed. For instance, artistic people are prone to imagine themselves as able to create great works, while they explain their inability to do so in practice by poverty, disease, and other rationalizations. The same applies to those people who are 'so spiritual'. They spend their time in keeping out of their mental and emotional auras all the impacts of life which are distasteful to them or which do not fit in with their fantasy part. Consequently, they live psychically isolated, in a bubble or on an island. The psychological impression they give people is that they are often charming and unusual people, but few suspect their remoteness. In contrast to this, the psychic impression is that there is no free and level exchange between themselves and others, except in a very limited field. They have a curious and subtle attitude of dispensing favours from an exalted plane, but they are unwilling to accept material at any level which displeases their over-fastidious taste. Instead of living in an all-round fashion, they separate off that part of their conscious life of which they approve into a watertight compartment, and push the rest into a relatively passive and unconscious state. This material contains energy, and therefore the potentiality of action. But by virtue of being locked away, the energy is held in a latent state, and has explosive possibilities in spite of being dropped out of sight. The psychic is often aware that behind the impressive façade of the personality there lurks something dangerous and terrifying.

If one analyses this impression further, one realizes that there is nothing in the consciousness of the person described to justify this fear. The mental aura is luminous and active, many of these people being highly intelligent and even creative. The emotional part, however, divides into two: light and pleasant feelings, which are bright and colourful, play through the emotional fabric, like sunlight and cloud-shadows on an April day. But the deeper and heavier emotions are not allowed any liberty and are kept in a state of suspended animation by the imposition of intellectual bonds. They hang like masses of coloured cumulus cloud save that they are caught in a network of imprisoning thought and are not free to drift across the emotional sky, but are anchored down to a comparatively static position.

The other variety of fantasy occurs in people who are really not interested in the world outside save perhaps where it affects their own comfort directly. They do not so much play a role in life as live in a cloud of self-absorption. The first type refuses to come to terms with his unconscious self, but has the power to impose himself on the world around in the guise of what he would like to be, and the world tends to accept him as such. This second type, however, makes no attempt to impress itself, but drifts through life in a psychic cocoon of its own weaving. It, too, is evading its unconscious problems, but if one asks, during a period of abstraction, 'What are you thinking about?' it answers, truthfully enough, 'I don't know. Of nothing.' The aura has a fuzzy, hazy outline which blunts the sharp edge of perception, and inside this blanketed aura the forms of thoughts and feelings wander aimlessly round and round, like goldfish in a cloudy bowl, resting nowhere and reaching no goal. Thus the victim is effectively prevented from seeing clearly either the world outside or the contents of his own mind.

Years spent living largely in fantasy tend to produce deterioration of the personality. The first type becomes increasingly artificial and the actor loses himself in the part he has chosen to play, so that the real person seems to withdraw and only a mask is left. Physical health may suffer from the attenuation of the vitality which flows when the real self is active. Consequently, the etheric bridge becomes tense and strained, like a piece of material pulled too tightly. Symptoms such as insomnia, rapid and tired heart, wasting conditions and anaemia, are apt to occur as a result of this. Such people have often a very lucid psychic sense and their artistic work has a quality of other-worldliness which gives it a particular appeal.

The second type, on the other hand, may become slack and soft, and there is an increasing likelihood of the victim becoming partly dissociated, falling into a half-way state in which he is focused clearly neither in the psychic nor in the physical world. The etheric fabric becomes loose and permeable, rather than rigid and brittle. In this state the individual may find himself obsessed by visions and dreams which do not belong entirely to the objective psychic world; nor do they emerge only from his own unconscious field. They are vague reflections of psychic phenomena seen at the mental and emotional levels, but because the focus is clear neither in the subjective nor the objective fields, the images presented are like those seen in a flawed and tarnished mirror. If this kind of person falls into the wrong hands he easily becomes a half-baked medium whose 'communications' are neither intelligent nor reliable. Many of these people find themselves troubled by uncontrollable emotions; they whirl like steam escaping under high pressure when anything unpleasant from outside really touches them, and produce scenes of hysteria and floods of tears and tantrums of temper, like any spoiled small child. They are also much open to sporadic clairvoyance or clairaudience which is quite out of their control and sometimes frightens them very badly. One woman of this type, a person with a good intelligence, was apt to throw herself on the floor in a fit of hysterical crying; when the sobbing died away her eyes were glazed, and it was often very difficult to awaken her from a half-trance state in which she might stay for hours. As she recovered from this condition, she sometimes found herself in psychic contact with people with whom she had an emotional link even when these were a very long way off, and was able to see what they were doing. Physical troubles are typically those of inertia, due to exhaustion of the sympathetic system. Their symptoms are such things as failure to digest and assimilate, colitis, constipation, low blood pressure, fatigue, and chronic infections such as occur in bladder and kidney.

The question which frequently puzzles psychologists is why a person unconsciously chooses a particular type of fantasy role out of many which would serve equally well as compensations and defences against everyday life. Heredity and early environment alone do not explain this. If we remember, however, that every child is born with certain individual behaviour patterns already established, and not to be traced entirely to physical heredity, we are on the track of a possible explanation. The child is already conditioned at birth by his past experience as an individual, which explains the particular psychological bias which makes and keeps him an individual, no matter how much or how skilfully his environment may be designed to mould him otherwise.

Thus one child, from his earliest days, shows an approach to life which is characteristic, let us say, of classical Greek training and culture. Another betrays the mask-like reticence and secretiveness of a Chinese monk, accepting life philosophically and yet with a certainty and tenacity of purpose which nothing can shake. A third has all the square-cut mentality of ancient Egypt. These basic attitudes are ineradicable: all that can be done is to develop as fully as possible in the present environment the capacities which lie within the framework of the pattern.

The particular fantasy adopted by an individual is likely to be founded on an exaggeration of the basic pattern, modified by present environment. The particular fantasy thus seems to have historic origin in the past experience of the individual, but he does not recognize that this historic past lies behind and is finished with. The momentum of it should, by rights, be carried forward without a break into the present day and the present environment, to which it must be fully adapted in order to lead to fresh experience. It is when this adaptation fails that the individual tries to perpetuate his old and familiar pattern in fantasy and play the role which is incongruous and out of touch with the realities of his present circumstances.

This accounts for the majority of so-called memories of past lives: they are so blatantly founded on wishful thinking that they are not worth taking seriously as of historical value, though they may serve a psychological purpose. It is, however, because of the grain of truth in such 'memories' that they are worth analysing as a guide to the fundamental psychology of the individual. It is, of course, not enough to explain present-day disgruntlements in terms of past experience, whether of this life or another, and the analyst needs to inquire as to the connection between that past and the present-day difficulties with a view to discovering the means of dealing with them here and now.

This is the psychological side of the picture. But it must be remembered that it includes the capacity for psychic perception as well as all other capacities. Past experience gives us our present capacities, and if we should have developed the psychic mechanism to a great extent in the past it would be the logical conclusion that we should be born with the same capacities latent but ready to spring into activity on being stimulated to-day. It is a fact that in past civilizations a great deal of attention was paid to psychic education, and many people to-day have good psychic powers for which present educational methods and social environment do not cater. This is the cause of much difficulty to them, as it leaves one side of their nature unexpressed and frustrated.

This is an important point to remember in cases of mediumship. The psychic capacities use energy exactly on a par with any other activity in the psychological field. These energies need to be allowed to express themselves freely. If represssed and disowned, they behave like any other complex and try and find their own outlet. The psychic, and especially the negative psychic, tends to be loosely knit together and easily acquires a habit of dissociation. Consequently, repressed psychic perceptivity may find itself projected into a dissociated part of the personality, where it becomes organized into what seems, even to the person of whom it is a part, to be a separate entity. This is the explanation of much of what is known in modern spiritualism as 'control'. There is evidence that the controlling 'spirit' is often a dissociated part of the medium himself. It is a part, however, which has a different range of perceptivity from that of the medium when not under control. If the control were to be integrated with the consciousness of the medium, the result would be a wide range of perception within the grasp of the single consciousness of the medium in his waking state. The fact that the alleged control may not be what it purports to be—i.e. a separate and discarnate person—does not imply either fraud or dishonesty on the part of the medium, nor does it diminish whatever value there may be in the communications received. Moreover, it does not exclude altogether cases of genuine control by people out of the physical body who have enough knowledge and capacity to make use of this method of communication with the physical world. But it is a method which, at best, must be a clumsy one. It would probably be far easier for a 'dead' person to communicate with the 'living' by means of telepathy.

It may be puzzling to those not versed in psychology to understand the rationale of the process, and why the medium needs to have an overshadowing control instead of giving his advice and messages directly and in full consciousness. There are at least four reasons for this, of which the first three are straightly psychological:

1. All psychics tend to be hypersensitive to criticism.

2. The dramatic instinct is strong in every human being; and what can be more dramatic than to be the chosen messenger of a spirit claiming deep mystical insight and having great gifts of wisdom with which to help the world?

3. A control absolves the medium from all responsibility and allows him to behave and say things in a way he would not dare to do in his normal state.

4. The half-way state of self-hypnosis in which the medium works actually enhances his sensitiveness by reducing the grip of material sensations on consciousness, and allows the wider but subtler field of the psychic world to be perceived.

In other words, a great deal of mediumship is psychologically based on compensative fantasy. But, by virtue of the element of psychic perception with which the fantasy 'control' is invested, the result is to produce objective results and phenomena which are perfectly genuine even though derived from a medley of sources.

The significant point about fantasy, then, is that it does not carry the individual from one place to another. He is not changed by it, but, on the contrary, he tends to perpetuate his old ways of thought and feeling, to retreat from objective reality and progress. In short, no matter how vivid fantasy may be and how much it affects the actions of the individual, it is a negation of experience, a buffer against facing unpleasant facts. It tends to diminish, not to increase, self-awareness, and to stultify, not to perfect and enlarge, a person's contact with life. It is consequently in direct contradiction to the laws of growth and evolution.

Not so the true imagination. This moves in open curves, not in closed circles, and the result of a train of imaginative thought is that the one who follows it grows by means of it. It does from within the mind what experience of external events does from outside it: it produces a change in the individual's awareness, in his attitude to life. The train of imaginative thought works on its own volition, and the observer only spoils it if he enters into it. In this way it bears a superficial resemblance to fantastic daydreaming. But in this case the observer remains, as it were, outside, watching the process as he might watch a film on a screen, and maintains an objective attitude to what is going on. If he does so, he may find himself led to a new awareness, and a new point of view about something he did not understand before. This does not always happen, as, frequently, he cannot hold his objectivity. He gets tired, perhaps, and the whole sequence becomes confused and broken before he reaches the end.

PERCEPTION, ETC.

On one occasion a man was sitting in a lecture hall listening to a speaker droning on at great length, and so dully, that he began to look for some way to relieve his boredom. On the wall there was a painted panel showing a terrace with a balustrade and, beyond, the outline of some trees. The man thought he would try a deliberate experiment in imagination, so he thought of himself as walking off the terrace and down to the trees in the background of the painting. He went down a path until he reached the trees, and when he got to them he found himself in a dip in the ground where there was a brook crossed by a little bridge. The picture was quite clear and vivid in his mind. He crossed the bridge, and continued along the path, which led him up towards high, snow-covered mountains. On the way, unexpectedly, he found a hermit's cabin and had conversation with the anchorite. The wise old sage, of whom he asked questions, gave quite unforeseen answers, and these he noted carefully, as both the substance and wording of them were not such as he would have habitually used himself. Then he crossed a high pass and went down the other side on to a glacier, where for a time he had to shelter behind a high ice-boulder from a snow squall. Then he crossed from the glacier on to firm ground again and entered a pinewood in which was a wooden cabin. In this, he knew, was somebody who meant a great deal to him. But by this time he was tired, and he lost his thread of continuity and could no longer objectify, so he got no farther. But he said that it was such a vivid and apparently objective occurrence that it stayed with him for days.

All of this can be interpreted in psychological terms, of course. But it was an experience of exploration by the use of the active imagination and it led to a certain change in the experimenter's mind. This was not merely because of the method he used, which was a piece of technique new to him, but because the journey represented a piece of actual psychological work and progress which lent itself usefully to analysis.

The point is that unconscious material had been evoked and brought to light by the use of imagination: it had been used as a means of research—in this case, into the man's own mind, the result being a series of symbolic pictures. But in other cases the imagination may help to evoke from the unconscious mind knowledge of external facts, perceived unconsciously, and registered in the 'forgetory' without having been consciously noticed at all. This is especially the case where psychic perceptions are concerned, since, as has already been pointed out, the perceptions of the psychic mechanism are so often obscured by the more clamorous physical world.

The technique of learning to use the imagination acquires a certain importance, therefore, in connection with the acquisition of conscious knowledge. For if a person can learn to ask himself a question and start from thence a train of imaginative thought, he may possibly find the correct answer by means of it—such an answer as he may subsequently be able to prove to be correct in the light of later observations, or which he may be able to go back to and check up by the slower road of logical or mathematical deduction.

One may suggest that most discoveries of importance may have been based on some such question as, 'I wonder if . . . ?' or 'I wonder how . . . ?' This might lead to a train of thought to the effect that if the point raised in the question was true, then certain other things would follow, and certain facts would be explained and fall into place. We do not know why or how Newton, who had probably seen thousands of apples fall to the ground, conceived the law of gravity. But it seems probable that, as a result of much work, there may have appeared in his mind some such question as, 'Suppose it was not the apple falling to earth, but the earth falling to the apple?' If this was so, then certain other phenomena could be explained by a general principle: the law of gravity, and its corollaries. In this case, the law could be checked by experiments which proved it correct—until a new genius imagined the principle of relativity, and proved the law of gravity to be only relatively true.

In psychic matters, the same accurate proof cannot usually be applied to what the imagination may suggest. But, nevertheless, if a light touch be used, it is both interesting and useful to experiment along the lines of imagination to try and discover what may be the psychic truth about a situation. And sometimes one will be surprised to find how one's imaginative forecasts of events, or one's estimate about a situation, is later proved accurate and true to the facts.

There is a story that Lord Rutherford was once being heckled by a tiresome philosopher as to the existence of electrons and other small particles of matter. He is said to have answered, 'Not exist? Why I can see the little beggars now!' Perhaps he did.

CHAPTER X

Insight

There is yet another aspect of perceptivity through which we gain knowledge and experience, and this is insight. Other names for the same thing are intuition and vision, if we refer to the knowledge aspect, while inspiration is the creative aspect; but the first name appears to be at once comprehensive and the clearest indication of what is meant. For to have insight means to see in depth, and not only superficially, to understand the real meaning of things and not merely their outward appearances. Without insight, no amount of learning, no amount of experience or experiment, is of any real value, because these are the husks of which insight is the kernel, the outside of the fruit of which insight is the creative seed:

This, however, is not to decry learning and experience: these have their essential part to play, and they create the conditions in which insight can be born. But insight alone gives that illumination which makes knowledge live.

It is of this that William Blake speaks when he says,

> '*To see a World in a Grain of Sand*
> *. . . And Eternity in an Hour.*'

This event is echoed in the following account. It is given by one who is a trained clairvoyant and therefore familiar with perceptive experience of both the physical and the psychic worlds. But what made this particular piece of perception exceptional was the addition to it of a whole range of implications which were evoked by, but were not themselves, what she saw.

'I was sitting on the seashore, half-listening to a friend arguing violently about a matter which merely bored me. Unconsciously to myself, I looked at a film of sand I had picked up on my hand, when I suddenly saw the exquisite beauty of every little grain of it: instead of being dull, I saw that each particle was made up on a perfect geometrical pattern, with sharp angles, from each of which a brilliant shaft of light was reflected, while each tiny crystal shone like a rainbow. The rays crossed and re-crossed, making exquisite patterns, of such beauty that they left me breathless.

'I was used, at odd intervals, to seeing the invisible counterpart of minute objects, but this was quite unexpected and fascinating. Then, suddenly, my consciousness was lighted up from within and I saw in a vivid way how the whole universe was made up of particles of material which, no matter how dull and lifeless they might seem at first sight, were nevertheless filled with this intense and vital beauty.

'For a second or two, the whole world appeared as a blaze of glory. When it died down, it left with me something I have never forgotten and which constantly reminds me of the beauty locked up in every minute speck of material around me.'

Such an experience is a very different thing from merely looking at an object, no matter how beautiful or interesting. After it, the one who has it is changed: something has happened to him and he is in some measure remade by it. It does not matter in what guise it takes place, nor how small the event which provokes it, but that sudden sense of complete knowledge of a situation brings about a transformation in oneself, in one's relation to the object one has just seen; and, in some cases, it also transforms the object itself. Charles Morgan defines the experience—save that he uses the word 'imagination' for what we have called insight—by saying that it 'consists in seeing things as they are—as they really are, their essences, not as they appear to be. It is the supreme realism of the spirit'.

Imagination, as described in the previous chapter, is not the same thing as insight. But insight may sometimes be found at the end of a flight of imagination, when it illumines the whole field. It may equally be found at the end of a train of logical reasoning. In all cases, the process starts from the material world of sense-perceptions and memories of sense-perceptions, traverses the field of consciousness, then seems to open a door at the opposite end from the material, to let in a shaft of light from the spiritual world. Here, knowledge is direct and complete, not partial and indirect, because it does not come through the limitations of the senses. Perception belongs to the world of time and space, but insight is timeless and spaceless. Perception is a relatively slow process, elaborate and intricate; insight is immediate and is essentially simple. Perception, being of parts, lends itself to synthesis: the building of fragments into a whole. Insight springs from a consciousness of wholes. But it can only be expressed in the language of the senses, which is analytical. Such language can never describe the whole, but only certain aspects of it—whence the inadequacy of words or any other means of expression to convey the truth. Perception is uncertain and open to doubt; it may be argued about. But true insight, in the moment when it is attained, gives quiet and flexible certainty which no amount of argument can shake: which is quite another thing from dogmatic tenacity and assertiveness. Perception often leads one into dark and tortuous ways, full of unexpected pitfalls and confusion. Insight, on the other hand, often gives one a vision of something so obvious that one marvels how one could have failed to see it before. Perception tells us what things look like, but insight is needed to tell us the truth of what they are. Imagination may be the bridge which links the two: that bridge on which man travels from time to timelessness and back again to time, bearing with him the fruits of the experience of a more than personal world. For perception is of the personal; insight belongs to the real Self.

It is on the return journey that the results of insight are to be seen. For true insight releases creative energy. This may take place at any level: if at the intellectual, it means a new current of scientific or philosophical thought; if at the emotional, it means an aesthetic experience; if at the physical, it results in really creative action, whether this be of a work of art or in any other department of life. A particular case is where a doctor, perhaps after many hours of work, gets a sudden view of his patient as a whole: not as a tiresome, sick personality, but as a spiritual being imprisoned by his own limitations. Neither party may be explicitly aware of what has happened, but it is the critical moment when healing occurs: the doctor sees his patient differently, and something within the patient also changes. He lets go of the old bad habits of thought and feeling to which he has unconsciously clung for so long, and begins to get well—or, in some cases, allows himself to die: which is sometimes the same thing as getting well, since it means release from the obsession of the disease-pattern.

In any case, the touchstone lies, not in the pleasure or even bliss of the experience, but in the greater creativeness it gives. Edward Carpenter summed this up when he said that if a person listened to great music and was not thereby made more energetic and creative, he had not *really* heard that music.

INSIGHT

The contrast between perception and insight suggests that they are opposite and complementary functions. They play into the field of consciousness from opposite ends. In fact, the polarity between them leads to the development of self-awareness. Insight, playing on to the consciousness of what is perceived, brings about the synthesis which gives these percepts meaning and makes us understand them; whereas perception, and the mental and emotional work which is done around perception, releases at the right moment the spiritual energy which gives that insight.

In this way, we may imagine the consciousness of man as lying between opposite poles of perception and insight. In that field things can happen because of the polarity, just as electricity can be generated in the field between the poles of a magnet. In the early stages of his development man's quest for knowledge was largely animal: to satisfy his needs. But, implicit and unconscious, there is in him the urge to go further, to seek knowledge as an end in itself, to become aware in the personality not only of the world around, but of himself; and, eventually, to perfect that awareness by uniting what he perceives explicitly with what he feels he already knows deep within himself. This deep knowledge is and must remain implicit and unexpressed until it is evoked into the conscious field prepared for it. And when it comes, it comes as a transforming and Pentecostal visitation and the start of a new phase in the mind of the individual who receives it.

Another analogy suggests itself, by which we may be able better to understand the difference between what we have called positive and negative psychism. For, if we consider the conscious field as a prism, positive psychism may be represented as a beam of white light falling on one side of it. As it goes through the prism it emerges, not as white light, but broken up into the colours of the spectrum: it is analysed out into the language of the senses.

If, however, we were to reverse the process and focus the coloured rays of the spectrum on to a point where they were synthesized, the result would be no longer colours but once more white light. In practice, however, the best one can do is to get something *nearly* white, because the coloured rays are affected by their passage through the air, and when they reach the point of focus they are no longer pure colours. This enables us to understand how it is that negative psychism is never absolutely accurate, however near the mark it may come. For the coloured rays stand for the different channels of sense-perception, the intervening air for the emotional bias of the percipient, and the point of synthesis for the place where he becomes conscious of them and identifies them as representing some object, physical or psychic. To have a really accurate view of the object, it needs to be seen in terms of white light— that is with insight, as against sense-perception alone. Then only is there a real certainty about one's knowledge. It is worth noting in connection with this analogy that various psychics agree on this point: that when they are working positively, what they see has about it a certain quality which they can only describe as 'whiteness' or 'radiance'—though the words are inadequate. One person summed the matter up by a paradox: 'It is as though what one sees is made up of white light of all colours.'

To leave the matter at this point, however, is misleading and mischievous. It is not possible for anyone to acquire positive psychic capacity without in the first place training himself to positive living in an all-round way. Positive psychism is part of the make-up of the spiritually developed person, and of nobody else. But it is only part of that make-up. A person may be spiritually developed, up to a point, and have very little perceptivity, either psychic or

physical. Inevitably, however, as he grows, his awareness
of the world outside his personality must also grow. The
Raja Yoga schools, as has already been said, understand
this fully. But they rightly deter the pupil from seeking to
develop psychic powers as an end in themselves: they
know too well the risk of developing any one aspect of the
individual while neglecting the rest. To do so leads to
monstrosities as if a man were to have a huge hand or head
on a dwarf's body, and the result is unbalance and ill
health.

To the Raja Yogi, 'siddhis', or psychic powers, are in-
cidental to the greater quest for truth. They come at the
proper time, and not before, to help the student on the
road to enlightenment. To develop them prematurely is
dangerous and foolish. But equally foolish is it to ignore
and not to use the powers which are one's own, whether
these be intellectual, bodily, or perceptive: for that is to
deny one's birthright, and this, too, leads to unbalance and
difficulty. Thus, between the Hatha Yogi who sets out to
develop psychic powers for their own sake, or for purposes
of wonder-working and sensationalism, and the Western
intellectual who tries to ignore whatever psychic capacities
he may have, there lies a middle and right way. This is to
learn to know oneself and one's capacities in every direction, and to use these to the full: not simply for emotional
satisfaction and to find new sensations, but in the search
for self-realization and truth. The quest for knowledge is
one thing, the quest for power and excitement quite another. The first leads to happiness and wisdom, the latter
only to suffering and distress.

But to seek wisdom, as against only accumulating
knowledge, needs a certain philosophical background, and
a sense of the purpose of life. This philosophy states that
man is essentially a spiritual being, who is learning to use

an animal mechanism as a means of apprehending and comprehending the material world to which that animal belongs. To achieve his purpose, man as a spirit—that which we have called the Self—needs to unfold that animal nature to its fullest extent, while adapting it to his own spiritual purposes.

In order to survive and reach his own needs, the animal has already developed to a high degree the power of physical sensitivity: the ability to respond to impacts from the outside physical world. This took place in response to the demands of instinctive desire—feelings, which supplied the energy required to do this. In the background, however, the animal also has a close and direct connection with the great sea of instinctive natural life, so that the individual animal is in touch with non-physical, or psychic, tides and currents. In other words, he has an inchoate unspecialized psychic sensitivity which motivates his outer activities.

Man, in addition to his animal nature, has an ever growing sense of self-hood, of I-ness. He wants to learn, to know, and this requires new faculties. The demand once more supplies the energy to develop these, and the result is that the rational powers of the mind gradually emerge. But he also needs new means by which to make contact with the world outside. The physical senses are already well-found, so he develops indirect methods of contact by means of apparatus. The psychic senses are not developed, they are vague and unformed, and consequently inadequate in relation to the dialectic powers of the intellect. So these senses need to be differentiated and made objective.

The purpose for which they are to be used must be the right one. That purpose is to help in the search for wisdom and understanding, and not to be used as a means of self-aggrandizement and gratification. A certain austerity of character marks the one who, not content with appearances, is searching for the reality of things. He is a person who is willing to submit to discipline: the discipline of learning to discard unessentials, whether these be material objects or habits of thought and feeling.

This brings us to the point where every true mystic, yogi, and occultist comes. It is a point common to every religion in the world, whether we consider Christian mysticism, Vedantic or Buddhist philosophy, or the traces of Egyptian-Hebrew mystery teaching which are still to be found in Freemasonry. In all of these the same lesson is taught: that no kind of perception is of use except as part of a deep urge to that self-realization which goes hand in hand with realization of the world about one. In this way only is balanced growth to be maintained, and the goal to be achieved.

To-day, in the West, man is turning increasingly towards the same goal. He knows where materialism has led him, how deceitful logic alone can be, and he is seeking new values. These are often intangible, unscientific, and to the materialist, unreal. But they are intensely vital and important to him.

Modern psychological tendencies are indicative of this. Starting from a nursery crudity, psychology is gradually working towards the idea that mysticism is right: that man can only be happy as he realizes himself, that the need for religion is intrinsic and basic, and that if properly understood by the individual, it represents an urge to live and grow, not a retreat from reality.

Man is looking for a vision of spiritual and eternal values, things which endure and are stable, no matter how much the material world may shift and change and collapse about his ears. But the spirit is an elusive thing, and every faculty of mind and body is required in the unending search for it. This and this alone is the true justification for learning to use psychic powers.

Appendix A

THE PSYCHIC CHILD*

Among the many books written, and in all the sound advice given about the difficulties and problems of childhood, there is little or nothing said about the psychic child: that is, one who is born with a degree of psychic sensitivity which nearly always lands him into trouble.

The child psychologist, whether that role be played by parents, teachers, or professional workers in the field, has the understanding of the child as an objective. Only too often, however, he has to discover the hidden causes which produce disharmony in the child's life. But often, with the best will in the world, he comes up against a blank wall, and there seems no good and sufficient reason why Mary, in the home of the Browns, is so totally different in her behaviour from the rest of the family. Granted that all the known psychological causes have been gone into, that everyone has tried to trace why Mary should be over-reactive to so many things, and why there should be elusive difficulties which are hard to pin down. At the end of it all, parents, teachers, and even the expert child psychologist cannot clear up the matter. Those willing to help are left feeling baffled by an undefinable quality in Mary that is extremely difficult, and that no assessment of this difficulty has been made.

Many cases of puzzling child psychology become reasonable and clear as soon as we recognize the nature of a child like Mary. This means facing the fact that the

* This article is reprinted by permission of *The Parents' Bulletin*.

events which influence her are not necessarily only those of the physical world, but that at times she may be responding unconsciously to external, though unseen, impacts made directly upon her psyche from an invisible world. These actually do motivate a lot of so-called senseless behaviour.

There are children who instinctively shun a crowd, or for whom every party ends in tears. These children are not necessarily the victims of ordinary shyness, nor of some terrifying experience. In some cases this may be so, but in others it is equally possible that the child is psychically sensitive (as many children normally are), and feels himself actually swayed hither and thither by the strong waves of emotional excitement which beat upon him from the crowd, and against which violence he is quite defenceless. The result of such experience to this type of child is exactly the same as though he were being buffeted by powerful waves upon the seashore, and the great difficulty of maintaining psychic equilibrium under such conditions corresponds exactly to the physical effort to keep one's feet.

A great deal of the distress of such a child is due to the fact that he cannot understand why he is so frightened and miserable. Every inquiry from his well-meaning elders only intensifies the hopeless struggle to bring the cause of his trouble into the field of expression.

This kind of problem is indeed difficult to understand and deal with unless one is aware that a child's sympathetic nervous centres are comparatively unguarded in the early years before the brain has taken control. These nerve centres play an important part in the psychic life, and psychic impacts such as those described above are genuinely shattering to these centres.

To-day there are numbers of children born with a degree of sensitivity which by its nature keeps them unprotected from much that heftier children neither see nor hear, and certainly do not respond to. These children may be either artistic or definitely psychic, but in each case the problems of adjustment to life are very similar. Many children are slightly clairvoyant in infancy or early childhood and grow out of it without ever having realized that they see more than their fellows; but the typically psychic child exhibits special traits to a marked degree: it is sometimes obvious that what to others is empty space is not so to him; he has a perception of objects which do not exist for other people; his link with colours, flowers, animals, etc., is very intimate, and his special response to them is apparent to close observers, though most often interpreted as being the result of a highly developed imagination. He often resents the disturbance arising from contacts with other children or his elders; they tend to break into his world with a ruthlessness which hurts and bewilders him since he has no idea that they do not sense or see the things with which he is so deeply occupied. Later on, when he *does* realize this, the knowledge often comes as a shock and causes deep concern.

Again, his sense of sound and touch is often acute, and he is apt to be nervously shattered by a sudden discordant noise, or if he is roughly handled; he hates to be picked up without warning, or embraced effusively; his overtense reaction to these experiences is sometimes met with by adult irritation, or attributed to surliness, and his parents and friends regard such behaviour as absurd and disproportionate to the circumstances.

Children of this order are often dreamers, and their private world is their most vivid possession. This world is real in part, for they may be either clairvoyant and actually see fairies, beautiful colours and lovely phenomena, or they may possess an extension of hearing and feeling which makes them alive to the reality of hidden things. But though the psychic child's special world is originally based upon his peculiar powers of perception, sooner or later fantasy creeps in and becomes inextricably mixed with reality. Hence confusion is bound to occur, and the child becomes difficult to manage.

Practically all psychically sensitive children are fastidious, and very difficult because of their hyper-sensitive reactions to most things, either at home or at school; they easily develop a temperature and obscure ailments without apparent reason; they are subject to sudden attacks of asthma, skin complaints, and frequent digestive upsets, and are very apt unconsciously to use these ailments as a means of escape from what is to them an insuperable difficulty—i.e. contact with people and places which are wholly alien to their inner world.

Children of this type are often not so much afraid of the dark, as of half-lights and shadowy corners in which they are always on the verge of seeing something alarming. These experiences are all the more terrifying because, in spite of their reality, they are formless and impossible to describe—yet they may often be the psychological cause of the many allergic ailments so common to their type.

In past generations these children have been a complete puzzle to most of their elders, but to-day we are at least intellectually aware of the fact of extra-sensory perception. It should therefore be easy to consider if a child's symptoms fit into such a psychological pattern as those I have described.

One thing is certain, that any child naturally possessing any marked degree of psychic sensitivity, is by nature of that capacity, bound to be an 'inconvenient' child. He will not fit into any orthodox pattern, and his moods and actions are likely to be unpredictable.

His nervous system is inevitably tense and over-reactive, and his response to everyday life tends to be different from that of his sturdier brother or sister. Ordinary affairs that are taken in their stride by the average child constitute for him peculiar difficulties. If this is not sufficiently understood by parents and teachers, he gets confused and bewildered. He feels at a disadvantage, and is entirely at a loss to explain his lack of ease. The discomfort in himself expresses itself in a number of apparently irreconcilable ways, and makes him awkward to deal with.

A great difficulty for parents and teachers trying to cope with these children is to learn to discriminate between ordinary misbehaviour and behaviour arising from some form of genuine extra-sensory perception. I remember an incident, slight in itself, which illustrates my meaning. Jennie, in her teens, was being talked to by a well-meaning grown-up. There was nothing condemnatory, nor critical, in the conversation. It was a friendly and ordinary conversation, but I saw that Jennie was on the verge of hysteria, and at the same moment I saw the reason for it. The aunt, in order to emphasize various points as she went along, was using her forefinger as a stabbing instrument, and at a range of about six inches from Jennie's body. Just as Jennie was about to wince physically and begin to cry, I said, 'Don't do that to Jennie, you are stabbing her aura, and hurting her!' A look of great relief swept across the child's face, and she flashed a brilliant smile of obvious gratitude to me. The aunt was puzzled and quite dismayed until I explained to her that as a child I had suffered desperately from such actions, and that they *did* actually hurt, but naturally unless one possessed a markedly psychic temperament, one could not possibly imagine or realize such a thing.

The problem for those in charge of such children is to

steer a middle course between paying too much attention and being over-anxious, or, on the other hand, being unsympathetic and dismissing unaccountable behaviour as nonsense. Parents of psychic children who encourage their sense of being wonderful, or too sensitive to cope with the hard corners of life can do very great harm, as they make the child feel 'special' and unusual. This leads on to unsocial, if not actually neurotic behaviour. The other end of the scale is equally disastrous. To be impatient, to try to harden such a child, or to laugh at it, only breeds resentment and hostility.

In fact, this problem is insoluble unless the grown-up person has some sound, even if slight, knowledge of psychology, and secondly, the power to make observations impersonally and objectively. This is extremely difficult if one is observing one's own child. Parents are seldom, if ever, free from anxiety. Pride, pleasure, what you will, creeps in with regard to their own children. Consequently there is, of necessity, an emotional colouring, or a personal bias in such observations. But to *really* help a psychic child, impersonality and friendliness, free from any tinge of anxiety or criticism, is essential.

It is not every psychologist who is clear about the distinction between psychological problems, and those arising from extra-sensory perception. A simple mode of expression is that what is a form of psychism (extra-sensory experience) is direct experience of external contacts at super-physical levels, while psychology is the study of the internal mechanism and motives of behaviour. To illustrate this at the adult level, let us take our response to music. When listening to music some people become emotionally affected by its vibration and their mood changes with the character of the music. Others, listening to the same music, immediately associate it with some episode of their life, and their response is governed by this association, and is not necessarily in accord with the music itself. The first response is psychic, the second psychological, and it is important to distinguish between the two because the mechanical action of the unconscious mind is entirely different. One is direct, due to the impact of external events, the other is indirect, the external event stimulating association and memories within the mind.

The child has less experience, but nevertheless behaves unconsciously in the same way. Suppose there is tension and strain between parents. The parents are careful to keep all appearances of their difficulties from the child. This does not in any way prevent the hypersensitive child from being deeply aware of the atmosphere of strain, and since he cannot know its cause, he becomes anxious and uncertain. This is his instinctive reaction to an external situation which he senses, and is exactly the same as it would be to a physical situation, fraught with danger, such as meeting a tiger in the woods. He could not describe the thing of which he is afraid, but he will probably express his fear indirectly. He may become rude and resentful to his parents in an attempt to defend himself from the atmosphere of conflict with which they surround him, he may turn his affections towards the charwoman who has a contented and placid nature, or he may develop night terrors, or regress into infantile habits like bed wetting.

There are no cut and dried rules for dealing with these problems, except one, which is to make the child feel psychically secure, and win his confidence. This cannot be done by any outward show, or an attempt to conceal from him one's own emotional stresses. Hence the essential thing in dealing with the psychic child is to be at peace within oneself. This can only be achieved through self-knowledge and self-understanding, and by facing one's problems and difficulties, and seeing them for what they are without pretence. It is useless for parents—if they want the best atmosphere for their children—to minimize or rationalize their personal problems or to cut them out by insisting they do not exist. It is also fatal to try to substitute home deficiencies by imposing a pious morality, or put before the child high-flown ideas of religion or idealism. All sensitive children are very quick to sense the hollowness of such substitutes.

If, on the other hand, the child can be induced to talk about himself, and what he senses or sees, with the assurance that he will be neither impatiently criticized nor ridiculed, half the battle will be won. It must be realized that psychic perceptivity is a very individual matter, and even if what the child says he knows does not fit in with the ideas of others, it is real, and hence, valid, to himself. One of the worst errors that can be made is to try and explain things away, or to say they cannot be like that, for, to a child, if to nobody else, they *are* like that, and must be accepted as such. The intuitive adult may find, however, the means of leading the child beyond his mixture of fantasy and psychic reality towards simple realistic values which will, nevertheless, harmonize with the truth which he has perceived.

For example, Mary seriously affirms that she has seen fairies while she has been out for a walk. This should be taken simply, and the question asked, 'What were they doing?' If there is no coherent reply, the constructive suggestion can be lightly made, 'Do you think they might be helping to grow the flowers and trees?' Or if May suddenly says she was very frightened after she was in bed, and it seemed as though someone was cross with her—if Father or Mother *was* angry or disturbed, it is better frankly and unemotionally to say, 'Yes! I am afraid I was upset—but it is all over now, and it certainly was not with you.'

It is this element of truth which gives the child both a feeling of security, and brings it into normal touch with the ordinary realities of life from which it is often only too anxious to escape.

In the modern world there are many of these children with us. A large number of them do not openly show their hypersensitive temperament, except in the form of dramatic ability, or some other line of artistic interest; but they are fundamentally open and responsive to many impacts of an unseen and unguessed at nature, and we have to learn to deal with them so that they may be happily adjusted to home and school life. These children particularly should never be allowed to get highly excited, or unduly tired. If signs of this are apparent, a quiet distraction and means of rest in the first place, and some barley sugar, glucose, or a hot drink in the second place are helpful.

The ideal environment for any baby, but more particularly for the sensitive child, is country life, with a minimum of being travelled around, and being shown off. At a later stage a small school is preferable to a large one, and in adolescence one in which the rougher games are not compulsory and forced on pupils, and in which there is plenty of scope for artistic expression, and quiet outdoor pursuits.

Such an ideal is clearly out of reach for most people, but the nearer the psychic and physical environment is to the ideal, the less the psychic child will suffer, and the more likely he is to grow up into a normal, if sensitive, adult.

Appendix B

FIRST AID

Every case of difficulty over psychic matters, like every psychological case, needs to be treated individually: the cause of the trouble is never twice the same, and to eradicate it requires re-education on individual lines. Nevertheless, certain general principles can be laid down, and simple suggestions made which may be of assistance. These must be looked on in the nature of first-aid rather than as likely to bring about a cure of the difficulty.

In general, cold, fatigue, anxiety and especially acute fear, disease and sedative drugs tend to slow the flow of vitality in the etheric body, while warmth, rest, hot drinks and food accelerate and increase it. This fact is particularly important to psychic people, who, under certain conditions, are apt to find themselves quite suddenly and unexpectedly exhausted and tired out. A short rest and a cup of hot coffee or tea will often lead to a rapid return of energy. Glucose or, for that matter, ordinary sugar, are specially valuable in such conditions.

While resting, the patient should be careful to relax his physical body thoroughly—without, however, dissociating and 'floating out'—and to remember to breathe properly.

Muscular relaxation is not an easy thing to learn. There are excellent books on the subject: Anne Payson Call's

APPENDIX B

Power through Repose, and Jacobson's *Progressive Relaxation* and the popular version of the same work *You Must Relax* give useful hints on the matter.

Breathing is a complex question, because it has deep-seated and far-reaching effects on the etheric bridge.

The physical mechanism by which the lungs are expanded, can be divided into two parts: one is where the volume of the chest is increased by raising the ribs, the other, where the same result is brought about by flattening the dome of the diaphragm, or midriff. In practice, if one is breathing deeply and easily, the two movements take place together.

In states of anxiety or uncertainty, there is a tendency for the diaphragm to be held stiff, so that the breathing becomes shallow and restricted principally to the upper ribs. Every markedly psychic person, moreover, tends to breathe badly and insufficiently—whence, perhaps, one of the reasons why they are so often in poor health and become easily tired.

To steady the etheric bridge, the student should learn to breathe freely and fully, but not too fully, and deeply, but not too deeply: if he overdoes this, the result is giddiness and discomfort. This is, of course, a good measure in general hygiene, quite apart from anything to do with psychic matters. The point is to learn to breathe with the diaphragm as well as the ribs. If one does this, the upper part of the abdominal wall is seen to move with the breathing, and the movement will not be restricted to the chest-wall alone. A useful way to achieve this is to breathe in, filling first the upper part of the chest, then the lower, then to breathe out from below first, emptying the upper part of the chest last. Gradually one should accustom oneself to this as a normal way of breathing. One may then perhaps become breathing-conscious, so that one realizes tension and anxiety because one feels the change of rhythm, and can then take steps to remedy it.

There is nothing elaborate about this, nor is there any comparison with the highly technical and complex breathing exercises of the yogis: it is merely a question of learning to use the physical mechanism correctly.

On the other hand, there is a much deeper significance to breathing than that of oxygenating the blood. The breath-rhythm corresponds with a systole and diastole—on the out-and-in breaths respectively—of the vital forces in the etheric body. It is on this co-ordination of psychic breathing with vital tides, that the yoga breathing systems are based. Thus, where psychic difficulties are concerned, it is sometimes found helpful if one carries in mind the suggestion that, on the in-breath one is gathering up vital energy and that on the out-breath it sweeps down through the etheric body, along every fibre of the nervous system, to the very tips of the fingers and toes. As it does this, it can be thought of as strengthening and harmonizing the whole of the fabric, cleansing it and driving out waste matter.

Sickrooms and hospitals are full of waste etheric material, and there are many other places which are psychically unclean. Negative psychics are apt to absorb this waste material and become contaminated with it. Some feel psychically depleted and physically exhausted, but others can feel positively ill as a result of this. A bath cleanses the etheric as well as the physical body, and some people find that the addition of sea-salt to the water has a particularly tonic effect on their bodies. In any case, warmth, fresh air, sunlight (in moderation) are excellent cleansers. To lie out of doors on a sunny day, with light and air playing on the skin, relaxed and breathing deeply and gently is an admirable means of re-creation.

Many people are extremely frightened of psychic invasion or, as it is commonly called, possession or obsession. There is no need for this: no psychic force or entity can invade the aura of a human being unless he himself opens the door to it. That is to say, in principle, that if a person's mind is positive, he is perfectly safe. If he becomes frightened, however, he is in a negative state, and he may then feel himself to be a prey to forces which do not seem to belong to him. But the 'entity' or force is almost certain to be really only an unconscious part of himself: something which psychological re-education can help him to deal with. Obsession, or possession by devils is—at any rate in western Europe—largely a myth.

In any case, if one realizes that one is master in one's own house, and that any intruder can be dealt with by positive thought and self-assertion, there is no need for fear. Indeed, it would be much easier to drive away an intruder coming from outside than to cope adequately with a dweller inside the house of one's personality, even though that dweller may hitherto have hidden himself away in the lumber-room of the unconscious mind.

It often happens that a person of mediumistic temperament becomes partly hypnotized by rhythmic movement or sound. He feels himself floating out of his body, going dreamy, and is in a half-way state or semi-trance condition. This may frighten him if he is not used to it; and, anyhow, it is not a desirable thing.

A positive physical action usually stops this: to move, to change one's position, to speak, or if none of these are convenient, to grip hard on the arm of one's chair and to evoke physical sensation may break the spell. But it must be remembered that the immediate phenomenon of dissociation rests on a fundamental temperamental negativity, and can be dealt with finally only by tackling the deeper aspects of the problem.

Such people will be wise to avoid any of the practices which involve a negative, receptive attitude, such as automatic writing, dowsing, the use of pendulums, and particularly, spiritualistic 'sittings'. This is not to deny that these methods are of value to some people. But, just as vigorous exercise may harm a weak heart, so are these practices bad for a person who tends to dissociate, because dissociation leads to uncontrollable impulses and sense-impressions such as hearing voices. These can be extremely troublesome.

A difficulty from which every sensitive person suffers is that due to noise, which bruises them or wears them down by a process of attrition.

No matter how sensitive one is, this is a thing which can be dealt with. If the mental attitude to noise is one of resistance, the result is to stiffen the etheric fringe, so that the sound-waves strike against it and cause repercussions in it. If the mental attitude can be changed, and noise is accepted as part of the scheme of things, like the weather, the battering ceases: a relaxation of psychic resistance immediately goes away with the tension in the etheric mechanism, and the sound, finding nothing on which to strike, passes harmlessly through the etheric fabric. This means, in practice, that the individual is no longer troubled by noise: he does not hear it willynilly, when he is otherwise occupied, and can get on with his task.

This brings out the important and fundamental principle that in all psychic matters, the psychological attitude is the determining factor.

Books Recommended

PSYCHICAL RESEARCH

These books approach the subject of psychic perceptivity from the scientific, evidential point of view. Only a few are listed here, though there are many others equally good.

Hereward Carrington, *Psychology in the Light of Psychic Phenomena*, *Problems of Psychical Research*
Gurney, Myers, and Podmore, *Phantasms of the Living*
Charles Richet, *Thirty Years of Psychical Research*
G. N. M. Tyrell, *Science and Psychic Phenomena*, *The Personality of Man*, *The Nature of Human Personality*
J. Sinel, *The Sixth Sense*
Eugene Osty, *Supernormal Faculties in Man.*
Society for Psychical Research, *Proceedings*

von Schrenck-Notzing, *Phenomena of Materialization*
J. B. Rhine, *Extra-Sensory Perception* (Statistical and Experimental), *The Reach of the Mind*, and other books
Whately Carington, *Telepathy*
P. D. Payne and L. J. Bendit, *This World and That*

AUTOBIOGRAPHICAL

Phoebe Payne, *Man's Latent Powers*
Eileen Garrett, *My Life as a Search for the Meaning of Mediumship*

BOOKS RECOMMENDED

PSYCHOLOGICAL

These books suggest indirectly the existence of psychic faculties, or link up with the hypotheses put forward in our text.

Frances Wickes, *The Inner World of Childhood*
W. H. Rivers, *Instinct and the Unconscious*
C. G. Jung, *Various books in which the collective unconscious is discussed*

ANIMAL PSYCHOLOGY

P. Marais, *The Soul of the White Ant*
M. Maeterlinck, *The Life of the Bee*
J. H. Fabre, *Wonders of Instinct* (also other books)

MISCELLANEOUS

Æ, *The Candle of Vision*
W. J. Kilner, *The Human Atmosphere* (research into the etheric double)
W. J. Dunne, *An Experiment with Time* (precognition in dreams, etc.)
Wilkins and Sherman, *Thoughts through Space*
Raynor Johnson, *The Imprisoned Splendour, Nurslings of Immortality*
Leslie D. Weatherhead, *Psychology, Religion and Healing*
Payne and Bendit, *Man Incarnate* (a study of the vital-etheric field)

Index